CONTENTS

P9-DFQ-831

Ministering in the Spirit and Strength of Jesus (A Study of 2 Corinthians, 1 and 2 Timothy, and Titus) is one of a series of study guides that focus exciting, discovery-geared coverage of Bible book and power themes—all prompting toward dynamic, Holy Spirit-filled living.

About the Executive Editor

JACK W. HAYFORD, noted pastor, teacher, writer, and composer, is the Executive Editor of the complete series, working with the publisher in conceiving and developing each of the books.

Dr. Hayford is Senior Pastor of The Church On The Way, the First Foursquare Church of Van Nuys, California. He and his wife, Anna, have four married children, all of whom are active in either pastoral ministry or vital church life. As General Editor of the *Spirit-Filled Life® Bible*, Pastor Hayford led a four-year project which has resulted in the availability of one of today's most practical and popular study Bibles. He is author of more than twenty books, including *A Passion for Fullness, The Beauty of Spiritual Language, Rebuilding the Real You*, and *Prayer Is Invading the Impossible*. His musical compositions number over four hundred songs, including the widely sung "Majesty."

About the Writer

PAUL McGUIRE is an author and speaker of increasing breadth of acceptance and demand, his ministry becoming noted for his spiritual sensitivity and forthrightness in addressing the New Age philosophy with practical and biblical wisdom. His local church and conference ministry effectively deals with pathways to restoring marriage, being healed from a broken past, and learning to minister to people in the New Age environment. His gift on these themes is enhanced by the way Paul confronts without condemning.

He was a student in psychology at the University of Missouri, and he now lives in Santa Clara, California, with his wife, Kristina, and their three children: Paul and twins Michael and Jennifer. The family is an active part of the congregation served by Dr. Hayford.

Paul McGuire's books include *Evangelizing the New Age, Supernatural Faith in the New Age, Marriage Breakthrough*, and *Healing from the Past*.

Of this contributor, the Executive Editor has remarked: "Paul is becoming a Holy Spirit instrument of pure and tender power in assisting victims in contemporary marital confusion and popularized error to come into spiritual liberty through Jesus Christ."

MINISTERING IN THE SPIRIT AND STRENGTH OF JESUS

A Study of 2 Corinthians,
1 and 2 Timothy, and Titus

Jack W. Hayford
with
Paul McGuire

THOMAS NELSON PUBLISHERS
Nashville

Ministering in the Spirit and Strength of Jesus
A Study of 2 Corinthians, 1 and 2 Timothy, and Titus
Copyright © 1998 by Jack W. Hayford

Published in Nashville, Tennessee, by Thomas Nelson, Inc.

All rights reserved. Written permission must be secured from
the publisher to use or reproduce any part of this book
except for brief quotations in critical reviews or articles.

Unless otherwise indicated, Scripture quotations are from the
New King James Version of the Bible, © 1979, 1980, 1982,
Thomas Nelson, Inc., Publishers.

Printed in the United States of America
1 2 3 4 5 6 7 8 — 03 02 01 00 99 98

THE GIFT
THAT KEEPS ON GIVING

Who doesn't like presents? Whether they come wrapped in colorful paper and beautiful bows, or brown paper bags closed and tied at the top with old shoestring. Kids and adults of all ages love getting and opening presents.

But even this moment of surprise and pleasure can be marked by dread and fear. All it takes is for these words to appear: "Assembly Required. Instructions Enclosed." How we hate these words! They taunt us, tease us, beckon us to try to challenge them, all the while knowing that they have the upper hand. If we don't understand the instructions, or if we ignore them and try to put the gift together ourselves, more than likely, we'll only assemble frustration and anger. What we felt about our great gift—all the joy, anticipation, and wonder—will vanish. And they will never return, at least not to that pristine state they had before we realized that *we* had to assemble our present with instructions *no consumer* will ever understand.

One of the most precious gifts God has given us is His Word, the Bible. Wrapped in the glory and sacrifice of His Son and delivered by the power and ministry of His Spirit, it is a treasured gift—one the family of God has preserved and protected for centuries as a family heirloom. It promises that it is the gift that keeps on giving, because the Giver it reveals is inexhaustible in His love and grace.

Tragically, though, fewer and fewer people, even those who number themselves among God's everlasting family, are opening this gift and seeking to understand what it's all about and how to use it. They often feel intimidated by it. It requires some assembly, and its instructions are hard to comprehend sometimes. How does the Bible fit together anyway? What does

Genesis have to do with Revelation? Who are Abraham and Moses, and what is their relationship to Jesus and Paul? And what about the works of the Law and the works of faith? What are they all about, and how do they fit together, if at all?

And what does this ancient Book have to say to us who are looking toward the twenty-first century? Will taking the time and energy to understand its instructions and to fit it all together really help you and me? Will it help us better understand who we are, what the future holds, how we can better live here and now? Will it really help us in our personal relationships, in our marriages and families, in our jobs? Can it give us more than just advice on how to handle crises? the death of a loved one? the financial fallout of losing a job? catastrophic illness? betrayal by a friend? the seduction of our values? the abuses of the heart and soul? Will it allay our fears and calm our restlessness and heal our wounds? Can it really get us in touch with the same power that gave birth to the universe? that parted the Red Sea? that raised Jesus from the stranglehold of the grave? Can we really find unconditional love, total forgiveness, and genuine healing in its pages?

Yes. Yes. Without a shred of doubt.

The *Spirit-Filled Life® Bible Discovery Guide* series is designed to help you unwrap, assemble, and enjoy all God has for you in the pages of Scripture. It will focus your time and energy on the books of the Bible, the people and places they describe, and the themes and life applications that flow thick from its pages like honey oozing from a beehive.

So you can get the most out of God's Word, this series has a number of helpful features. Each study guide has no more than fourteen lessons, each arranged so you can plumb the depths or skim the surface, depending on your needs and interests.

The study guides also contain six major sections, each marked by a symbol and heading for easy identification.

WORD WEALTH

The WORD WEALTH feature provides important definitions of key terms.

BEHIND THE SCENES

BEHIND THE SCENES supplies information about cultural beliefs and practices, doctrinal disputes, business trades, and the like that illuminate Bible passages and teachings.

AT A GLANCE

The AT A GLANCE features uses maps and charts to identify places and simplify themes or positions.

BIBLE EXTRA

Because this study guide focuses on a book of the Bible, you will find a BIBLE EXTRA feature that guides you into the Bible dictionaries, Bible encyclopedias, and other resources that will enable you to glean more from the Bible's wealth if you want something extra.

PROBING THE DEPTHS

Another feature, PROBING THE DEPTHS, will explain controversial issues raised by particular lessons and cite Bible passages and other sources to which you can turn to help you come to your own conclusions.

FAITH ALIVE

Finally, each lesson contains a FAITH ALIVE feature. Here the focus is, So what? Given what the Bible says, what does it mean for my life? How can it impact my day-to-day needs, hurts, relationships, concerns, and whatever else is important to me? FAITH ALIVE will help you see and apply the practical relevance of God's literary gift.

As you'll see, these guides supply space for you to answer the study and life-application questions and exercises. You may, however, want to record all your answers, or just the overflow from your study or application, in a separate notebook or journal. This would be especially helpful if you think you'll dig into the BIBLE EXTRA features. Because the exercises in this feature are optional and can be expanded as far as you want to take them, we have not allowed writing space for them in this study guide. So you may want to have a notebook or journal handy for recording your discoveries while working through this feature's riches.

The Bible study method used in this series revolves around four basic steps: observation, interpretation, correlation, and application. Observation answers the question, What does the text say? Interpretation deals with, What does the text mean?—not with what it means to you or me, but what it meant to its original readers. Correlation asks, What light do other Scripture passages shed on this text? And application, the goal of Bible study, poses the question, How should my life change in response to the Holy Spirit's teaching of this text?

If you have used a Bible much before, you know that it comes in a variety of translations and paraphrases. Although you can use any of them with profit as you work through the *Spirit-Filled Life® Bible Discovery Guide* series, when Bible passages or words are cited, you will find they are from the New King James Version of the Bible. Using this translation with this series will make your study easier, but it's certainly not necessary.

The only resources you need to complete and apply these study guides are a heart and mind open to the Holy Spirit, a prayerful attitude, and a pencil and a Bible. Of course, you may draw upon other sources, such as commentaries, dictionaries, encyclopedias, atlases, and concordances, and you'll even find some optional exercises that will guide you into these sources. But these are extras, not necessities. These study guides are comprehensive enough to give you all you need to gain a good, basic understanding of the Bible book being covered and how you can apply its themes and counsel to your life.

A word of warning, though. By itself, Bible study will not transform your life. It will not give you power, peace, joy, comfort, hope, and a number of other gifts God longs for you to unwrap and enjoy. Through Bible study, you will grow in your understanding of the Lord, His kingdom and your place in it, but you must be sure to rely on the Holy Spirit to guide your study and your application of the Bible's truths. He, Jesus promised, was sent to teach us "all things" (John 14:26; cf. 1 Cor. 2:13). So as you use this series to guide you through Scripture, bathe your study time in prayer, asking the Spirit of God to illuminate the text, enlighten your mind, humble your will, and comfort your heart. He will never let you down.

My prayer and goal for you is that as you unwrap and begin to explore God's Book for living His way, the Holy Spirit will fill every fiber of your being with the joy and power God longs to give all His children. So read on. Be diligent. Stay open and submissive to Him. You will not be disappointed. He promises you!

Lesson 1/ The Apostle Paul's Mission Impossible
(2 Corinthians 1:1—2:11)

The apostle Paul faced a seemingly impossible mission. God had called him to plant a church in first-century Corinth, a leading commercial center of southern Greece. It was a "wide-open boomtown" similar to San Francisco of the gold rush days. The church was filled with new converts saved out of the pagan world of Corinth, famous for its immorality and loose living. Like any cosmopolitan city, Corinth was a mixture of different races and cultures, and the Corinthian church had its difficulties with factions and instabilities.

To compound problems, Paul had to deal with false teachers and people struggling for power in the church. In this seemingly impossible context, God placed Paul not only to plant but to continue to oversee a church. His experiences, as they are expressed through this letter, offer anyone called into ministry at any level the rare opportunity of observing how a ministry under fire continues in the Spirit and strength of Jesus.

Far from being recognized as a kind of "superstar" of the faith in his own time, 2 Corinthians shows Paul to be a down-to-earth apostle who faced challenges in ministry similar to those we face today. Paul was not an unapproachable or holier-than-thou saint. Like us, he had weaknesses and personal struggles. Neither, as we shall see, was Paul everywhere revered and given the red-carpet treatment we today might think every church would roll out for this great apostle. On the contrary, Paul was in some respects so utterly human, so merely normal, that some super-spiritual believers disdained and dishonored him. These were mesmerized by style over substance, and in their disappointment at not finding the ministry style they wanted in Paul, they failed to recognize that

Paul was representing Jesus Christ to and among them most faithfully.

Paul's response to these challenges demonstrates how God delights in expressing His strength through human weakness. This divine choice is expressed clearly in the cross of Jesus and also, in a way that is practical for believers and spiritual leaders today, in the experience and example of Paul.

AN OVERVIEW OF 2 CORINTHIANS

After reading "Behind the Scenes" and scanning the following table on 2 Corinthians, read the entire epistle quickly.

BEHIND THE SCENES

Read the references given with each item in the sequence below. Note the events that led up to the writing of 2 Corinthians.

PAUL'S DEALINGS WITH THE CORINTHIAN CHURCH, A.D. 50–56

1. The *founding visit* to Corinth (A.D. 50) lasted approximately eighteen months (see Acts 18).

2. Paul wrote an *earlier letter* before 1 Corinthians (see 1 Cor. 5:9).

3. *First Corinthians* was written from Ephesus around A.D. 55.

4. A brief but *painful visit* to Corinth resulted in sorrow for Paul and the church (see 2 Cor. 2:1; 13:2).

5. Shortly after the painful visit, Paul wrote a *severe letter,* which was delivered to Corinth by Titus (see 2 Cor. 2:4; 7:6–8).

6. Paul penned *2 Corinthians* from Macedonia (probably A.D. 55 or 56), while on his way to Corinth again.

7. Paul's *last visit* to Corinth (Acts 20) was likely when he wrote Romans, just before returning to Jerusalem.

The painful visit and the severe letter provide the immediate background for the writing of 2 Corinthians.[1]

From your reading, complete this overview table with the information requested:

SECOND CORINTHIANS

Type of Book:	Date Written:		
Author:	**Recipients:**		
Repeated Words or Ideas:	1:1–11 1:12—7:16 8—9 10—13		
Points from Key Verses:	1:12; 2:17; 3:5, 6; 4:1, 2; 5:9–12; 6:1, 3–10; 7:2, 3; 8:10, 11; 10:7–18; 11:1–5, 16–21; 12:14–21; 13:1–6		
Purpose for Writing:	First Corinthians did not resolve all the problems at Corinth. Certain people there continued to resist Paul's leadership and to		

threaten to control the church. These had worldly ideas of what a strong spiritual leader should be like. Other Jewish Christian missionaries also came to Corinth, were better liked by the worldly-minded among the Corinthians, and usurped Paul's authority as apostle to and spiritual father of this church. Through 2 Corinthians, Paul seeks to bring the church back to the loyalty proper to him, to the gospel, and to Jesus and to cause them to renounce their destructive loyalty to opponents, the "false apostles." Through this letter, Paul contrasts ministry that is true to the spirit of Jesus and that is sustained by His strength against ministry that expresses a worldly, self-serving spirit and that is sustained by worldly ideas of strength and power.

COMFORTED TO BE A COMFORT (2 COR. 1:3–11)

A recent poll among evangelical Christian pastors revealed that a significant percentage of those in the ministry felt emotionally isolated and discouraged, doubted their call to ministry, and considered leaving it. Paul's response to the serious difficulties at Corinth points spiritual leaders and all believers to the resource that will sustain them in any challenge.

How does Paul name this Source of strength and encouragement? (1:3, 4)

WORD WEALTH

Comfort *(paraklēsis)* means a calling alongside to help, to comfort, to console or encourage. The *paraklete* is a strengthening presence, One who upholds those appealing for assistance. *Paraklēsis* (comfort) can come to us both by the Holy Spirit (Acts 9:31) and by the Scripture (Rom. 15:4).[2]

Paul was commissioned by God to be an apostle, an assignment he was able to fulfill only by knowing the reality of the *paraklete* and understanding the God of all comfort. By properly defining the concept of "comfort," we can understand how we live the Christian life, which is impossible in merely human strength and wisdom.

Read 2 Corinthians 1:3, 4 and Acts 9:31 and note how "comfort" is used. Then write three different means God can use to comfort us.

1.

2.

3.

What is one positive result of being "comforted by God"? (1:4)

Now read John 15:26, and write why the comfort of God is personal. Describe the role the Holy Spirit plays not only in helping us, but also in comforting us.

 BIBLE EXTRA

Paul teaches us that the God "who comforts us in all our tribulation" (1:4) strengthens us supernaturally. The secret of Paul's strength was written by Isaiah the prophet around 700 to 690 B.C., when the Spirit of the Lord spoke through him saying, "But those who wait on the Lord shall renew their strength; they shall mount up with wings of eagles, they shall run and not be weary, they shall walk and not faint" (Isa. 40:31).

Both Paul and Isaiah wrote about ordinary believers or Christian leaders seeking the presence of the Lord in the midst of the demands and pressures of life. His presence consoles, comforts, and strengthens. From this place of rest and delight with the Lord, the fountainhead of true ministry rises. Comforted by the Lord, believers can comfort others.

Although God can and does comfort people directly through His Holy Spirit, why do you think it is important that we encourage one another? (1:4)

Why is it vitally important that we find practical ways to honor, uphold, and even defend (if need be) our pastors and the other spiritual leaders God has placed in our lives? (1:3–5, 5–7, 8–11; 11:23–29)

ANSWERING THE CRITICS: COMPLAINTS AGAINST PAUL (2 COR. 1:1, 2; 1:12—2:2)

Paul's commission as an apostle was one of the key issues of this letter. First Corinthians did not fully solve the problems of the church at Corinth. Among these, there appears to have been a man opposing or otherwise trying to usurp Paul's authority. (This situation is referred to in 2 Corinthians 2:4–8, in which Paul refers to another letter to the Corinthians, which has been lost.) This challenge to Paul's leadership persists and worsens, so much so that the final chapters of 2 Corinthians (10—13) focus on this issue. In the whole letter, but especially in these chapters, Paul identifies the essential qualifications of ministry in the Spirit and strength of Jesus. Second Corinthians reveals the depth of Paul's commitment to Christ, his painfully deep love for the believers at Corinth, and his righteous indignation at those who remake Jesus and the gospel according to worldly ideas. In 2 Corinthians, we see a New Testament portrait of a leader who, like Jesus Christ, gave himself completely for the church.

On what basis did Paul receive his authority to be an apostle of Jesus Christ? (1:1)

Paul responds to criticisms and serious challenges to his ministry throughout the letter, so he wants the beginning of the letter to encourage the Corinthians to feel a close bond with him. From each of the following references, write the words that show that Paul and the Corinthians are, or can be, tied closely to each other.

vv. 3–4

vv. 5–6

v. 7

vv. 10–11 (but read vv. 8–9 too)

As he will do later in the letter, Paul both pictures himself and the Corinthians in a relationship of mutual benefit, and he also invites them to participate more fully.

In verse 13 Paul responds to the first of several criticisms leveled against him. Read verses 12–14, then list that criticism here:

As we proceed through this study, we will see that the criticisms and challenges to his leadership forced Paul to boast of his ministry and its accomplishments in order to protect the church from destructive leaders who would exploit it. In fact, 2 Corinthians speaks more than any other New Testament book about boasting (see 1:12, 14; 5:12; 7:4, 14; 10:8, 13, 15–17; 11:10, 12, 16–18, 30; 12:1, 5, 6, 9).[3] Here (v. 12)

Paul boasts, in terms similar to courtroom testimony, that his conduct has been fully aboveboard. "Simplicity" means "straightforwardness," or "without duplicity." Paul feels the need to emphasize similar points later too. Fill in the terms from later in the letter (10:1–5; 12:11–13) that correspond with these terms from 1:12:

"conducted ourselves in the world"	"not with fleshly wisdom"	"by the grace of God and more abundantly toward you"
_____	_____	_____
10:3	10:4	10:1; 12:11–13

In 1:14, how does Paul again seek to strengthen the bond between him and the Corinthians?

Paul responds to a second criticism in 1:15—2:2. Read this section to identify the complaint (paying special attention to 1:15–18), and write it below:

Note Paul's use of expressions that include "flesh" with a negative meaning. Write out the "flesh" expression that occurs in each of the following references, and then write what you think is the opposite of each expression:

Reference	"Flesh" expression	Its Opposite or Alternative
1:12		

1:17

10:2, 3

At the core of integrity, of straightforwardness, is character—being people of our word, people whose "yes" means simply "yes" and not "yes and no" at the same time. Fickle people are not stable; they do not have integrity and can't be counted on to lead or follow reliably. Paul has been accused of such fickleness here, because he said he would visit the Corinthians but then changed his mind. Study the following references together to determine why Paul changed his mind, and write that below:

1:15, 16

1:23

2:1–8

AT A GLANCE

Study the map "The Life of Paul" on the next page, and circle the places mentioned in 2 Corinthians 1:15, 16 (Jerusalem is in Judea). Draw lines with arrows among them showing the itinerary Paul planned, but did not keep at that time.

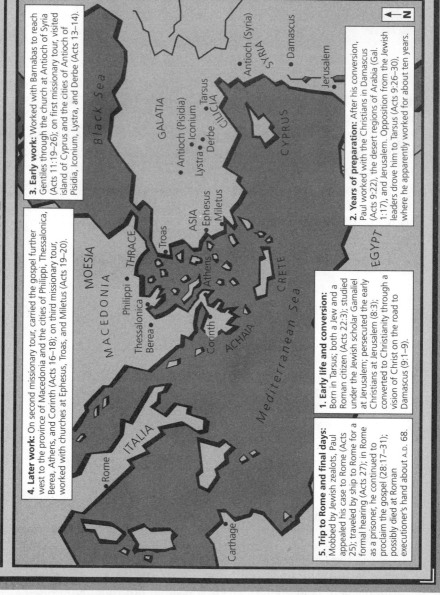

THE LIFE OF PAUL[4]

1. Early life and conversion: Born in Tarsus; both a Jew and a Roman citizen (Acts 22:3); studied under the Jewish scholar Gamaliel at Jerusalem; persecuted the early Christians at Jerusalem (8:3); converted to Christianity through a vision of Christ on the road to Damascus (9:1–9).

2. Years of preparation: After his conversion, Paul worked with the Christians in Damascus (Acts 9:22), the desert regions of Arabia (Gal. 1:17), and Jerusalem. Opposition from the Jewish leaders drove him to Tarsus (Acts 9:26–30), where he apparently worked for about ten years.

3. Early work: Worked with Barnabas to reach Gentiles through the church at Antioch of Syria (Acts 11:19–26); on first missionary tour, visited island of Cyprus and the cities of Antioch of Pisidia, Iconium, Lystra, and Derbe (Acts 13–14).

4. Later work: On second missionary tour, carried the gospel further west to the province of Macedonia and the cities of Philippi, Thessalonica, Berea, Athens, and Corinth (Acts 16–18); on third missionary tour, worked with churches at Ephesus, Troas, and Miletus (Acts 19–20).

5. Trip to Rome and final days: Mobbed by Jewish zealots; Paul appealed his case to Rome (Acts 25); traveled by ship to Rome for a formal hearing (Acts 27); in Rome as a prisoner, he continued to proclaim the gospel (28:17–31); possibly died at Roman executioner's hand about A.D. 68.

"Be helped by you on my way to Judea" (1:16) refers to Paul's desire to make two trips to Corinth. On the second trip, Paul wanted to collect a financial gift from the Corinthians that would cover his travel expenses and provide a generous offering for the poor saints at Jerusalem. Chapters 8 and 9 show that the poor saints of Macedonia had already contributed to this gift (8:1–4) and that Paul wanted the financially better-off Corinthians to contribute as well. This gift responded to the poverty of Jewish believers at Jerusalem, but, more importantly, it aimed to strengthen the bonds of fellowship between Asian and Judean Christians, between churches largely Gentile in make-up (the Philippian and Corinthian churches) and the "mother church" of Jews in Jerusalem.

Verses 18–20 shore up Paul's claim to integrity—not fickleness. In each of the following verses, what is not "Yes and No" but "Yes" only?

v. 18

v. 19

v. 20 (not "Yes and No" is implied)

What acts of God that the Corinthians have experienced does Paul cite in verse 22 as further proof that God is not fickle, not "Yes and No," when it comes to keeping His promises?

Paul's critics said that by changing his mind and not visiting them as he had intended to do, he has shown himself to be an untrustworthy promise-breaker. Review verses 18–22, and express in your own words Paul's answer to his critics.

In verses 21–22 Paul lists four actions of God that Paul and the Corinthians have jointly experienced. List them here:

1.

2.

3.

4.

The first of these terms here marks God's continuing activity: "He who establishes [or confirms] us with you." The others are expressed in verbs that refer to God's past action, the basis for His continuing action of confirming to believers that they continue to belong to Him and He to them.[5]

WORD WEALTH

Guarantee (1:22) (from *arrabon,* Strong's #728) is a business term that speaks of earnest money, a part of the purchase price paid in advance as a down payment. *Arrabon* is the first installment, which guarantees full possession when the whole is paid later. Sometimes this transaction was called "caution money," "a pledge," "a deposit," "a guarantee." *Arrabon* describes the Holy Spirit as the pledge of our future joys and bliss in heaven.[6] Revelation 21:4 describes a time when there will be no more death, sorrow, crying and pain. Revelation 21:22–26 portrays heaven as a place where the glory of the Lord will give us all the light we need and we will not need light from the sun or moon. The Holy Spirit now gives us a foretaste or guarantee of such things to come.

How does the Holy Spirit in our hearts as a guarantee enable us to overcome adversity and challenges in ministry? (1:22)

How does this "foretaste of glory divine" make it possible to proclaim the reality of Christ's resurrection to an often hostile and unbelieving culture?

How should this "Spirit in our hearts as a guarantee" affect our emotional state when we like Paul see trouble coming from every direction? (1:22)

Identify the third complaint against Paul in 1:23—2:4, and write it below. Note that Paul denies this complaint specifically in 1:23.

List the words from this passage that Paul uses to guarantee the truthfulness of his explanation. These are words that might be uttered in a courtroom.

Summarize Paul's explanation for his change in travel plans. (2:1–3)

DISCIPLINING THE DISOBEDIENT AND DISRESPECTFUL
(2 COR. 2:3–11)

Church discipline may be the most difficult of all tasks for a minister and a church. It is challenging enough when a member's error is persistent, flagrant sin of which the broader community becomes aware. But the case Paul has to deal with is even thornier. In addition to the three complaints expressed in the preceding passages of 2 Corinthians, 1 Corinthians 4:18

and 9:1–18 show that some at Corinth claimed Paul was never coming back and that some suspected Paul's motives for ministry because he declined financial support and worked to support himself. Clearly, Paul's relationship with this church was deteriorating, and he visited Corinth (before the writing of 2 Corinthians) to try to patch things up. Instead, this visit was painful for Paul and for the Corinthians. During that visit, someone at Corinth directly challenged Paul's authority, insulted him, and demanded that he prove that Christ was working through him (2 Cor. 13:3). To make matters worse, the rest of the congregation did not immediately support Paul in this conflict.

PROBING THE DEPTHS

In 2:3, 4, Paul mentions the *severe letter* which followed the *painful visit.* Although some identify the entire epistle of 1 Corinthians or 2 Corinthians 10—13 as that letter, neither seems to fit the description, and manuscript evidence gives no valid reason to separate chapters 10—13 from the rest of the epistle. Both the painful visit and the severe letter appear to involve resolving a challenge to Paul's apostolic authority (see 2:3–11; 7:6–13).[7]

Read 2:3–11 and 7:6–11. How did the Corinthians show obedience to Paul?

What words in 2:5 show Paul's continuing effort to help the Corinthians see that they and he are "in this together," as we might say today, that an offense against him was at the same time an offense against them?

What further obedience does he hope will bring him joy when he visits? (2:6–10)

What evidence do you find in this passage that not everyone at Corinth agreed with the discipline meted out to the offender? (2:5–11)

What "two sides of love" are involved in balanced discipline and mutual accountability? (2:3–10)

 BIBLE EXTRA

In this passage, Paul directs the Corinthians to stop disciplining the one who opposed him. Paul discerns that further discipline would only harm the offender and not lead to his restoration; and restoration—not punishment itself—is the goal of godly discipline. Compare 2 Corinthians 2:5–11 with the following other passages that deal with church discipline. Note where they give similar instructions and also where they include something additional.

Passage	How similar to 2 Cor. 2:5–11	How different from 2 Cor. 2:5–11
Matt. 18:15–18		
Gal. 6:1		
1 Tim. 5:1, 2, 19, 20		
Titus 1:10–13; 3:10–11		

Read the context surrounding these other passages to be sure you understand how the specific verses fit the larger message. Then, based on these passages, pull together a summary statement on how a church should approach discipline, and write it below. Imagine that you will offer the statement for church leadership to consider as they draft policy for a local church.

By working through this lesson, how have your thoughts changed about what ministry was like for the apostle Paul?

What one to three new insights or bits of information stand out in your mind?

How does what you have learned so far affect how you feel about the challenges you face in your ministry?

About your opportunity and responsibility to support and be loyal to fellow ministers and those in responsibility over you?

FAITH ALIVE

In 2 Corinthians 1:1—2:11, Paul says more than we might realize at first about what true spirituality is. These verses may cause us to feel inadequate, even a little frightened about the call to a deeper discipleship that is outlined here. After reviewing this chapter write down the areas where you may be experiencing challenges, afflictions, tribulations, suffering, and difficulty. Next, write how you believe the Holy Spirit can help you and give you the power to be the kind of person God wants you to be regardless of the circumstances.

Areas of Trial and Difficulty	How the Holy Spirit Can Help Me in These Circumstances

After you write these things down, spend some time in personal prayer in which you . . .

- Commit these circumstances to God.

- Thank God for His power and blessing at work in your life.

- Praise Him for strengthening you and helping you in the midst of your circumstances.

- Cast the burden of these circumstances over to Him and trust Him to work all these things out.

1. *Spirit-Filled Life® Bible* (Nashville: Thomas Nelson Publishers, 1991), 1749, "Background and Date, 2 Corinthians."

2. Ibid., 1643, "Word Wealth: Acts 9:31, comfort."

3. Linda L. Belleville, *2 Corinthians: IVP New Testament Commentary Series* (Downers Grove: InterVarsity Press, 1996), 61.

4. *Word In Life Study Bible* NKJV (Nashville: Thomas Nelson, 1996), 2002.

5. Belleville, 67.

6. *Spirit-Filled Life® Bible*, 1753, "Word Wealth: 2 Corinthians 1:22, guarantee."

7. Ibid., 1753–1754, Notes on 2 Cor. 2:3, 4, 5–11.

Lesson 2/Ministering Triumph in Christ through Integrity
(2 Corinthians 2:12—3:18)

Perhaps you have heard of the old expression, "I have been down so long, everything looks up to me"; or "If life's a bowl of cherries, why do I feel like I'm in the pits?" Both of these expressions reflect a deep weariness, even despair, that many feel today. If not responded to properly, disappointment, tragedy, hurts, rejections, lost opportunities, and setbacks can produce a cynical and negative state of mind that is not biblical. The apostle Paul was clearly no stranger to difficulty and disappointment. Yet, in the midst of adversity, Paul thanks the God "who always leads us in triumph in Christ" (2 Cor. 2:14).

For the person who knows God through Jesus Christ, "God always leads us in triumph in Christ" (2:14). Notice the "always" (v. 14). Does this important adverb mean that things will always go our way or that we will never experience defeat, disappointment, or failure? No! But it does mean that if we are in Christ, we will always come out on top spiritually, and we will be victorious.

Such triumph transcends mere positive thinking or simply keeping a good attitude. Paul understood the adversity in his life in the greater context of God's master plan for him. As such, he realized that as he continually sought the Lord, God was ordering events behind the scenes for his good. Paul did not become "fatalistic," nor did he "roll over and play dead" in the face of adverse circumstances. Paul "fought the good fight of faith" and employed powerful spiritual weapons. But, most of all, Paul was empowered by the Holy Spirit. He was open to and walked in the presence of God, and the resurrection power of Christ carried him through circumstances that humans would not endure through their own strength.

Yes, Paul faced the same temptations, feelings of frustration, anxiety, fatigue, and discouragement that you and I may face. But he learned how to take these things to God in prayer and to allow Jesus Christ to strengthen him from within.

ISSUES OF LIFE AND DEATH (2:12–17)

Using the map below, trace the travels Paul describes in verses 12 and 13.

    AT A GLANCE

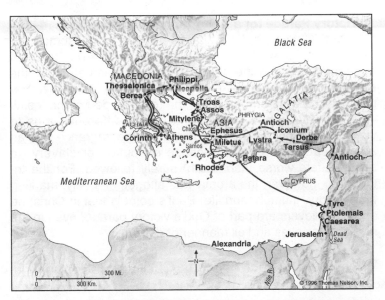

ASIA AND GREECE REVISITED (PAUL'S THIRD MISSIONARY JOURNEY, ACTS 18:23—21:16)[1]

Paul visited the churches of Galatia for a third time, and then settled in Ephesus for more than two years. Upon leaving Ephesus, Paul traveled again to Macedonia and Achaia (Greece) for a three-month stay. He returned to Asia by way of Macedonia.

On his third journey Paul wrote 1 Corinthians from Ephesus, 2 Corinthians from Macedonia, and the letter to the Romans from Corinth.

What information in 2 Corinthians 2:12–17 concerning Paul's detour to Troas responds to the earlier criticism that Paul is fickle, that he changes his traveling plans on a whim?

If some of the Corinthians persist in doubting Paul's care for them, how might his telling about his anxiety over Titus help change their minds? (2:13)

BEHIND THE SCENES

A Victory Parade for a Conquering Army (2 Cor. 2:14–16)
    In this passage, Paul may be alluding to the Roman victory parade that was common in his day. In this parade, both the conquering and the defeated leaders marched down the street, along with the victorious army and their captives. Fragrant spices were burned along the route as part of the festivities. However, the same aroma meant different things to victor and vanquished. To the defeated, the fragrance was an aroma leading to death, because execution or slavery (to some, a fate worse than death) surely followed. For the triumphant, however, the aroma was altogether lovely, marking their victory, triumph, and life. Paul's point is that in Christ he and all believers are part of God's victory parade, even in the midst of anxieties and all manner of difficulty.

Why is the gospel of Jesus Christ the aroma of life to those who are being saved? (2 Cor. 2:15–16)

Why is the gospel the aroma of death to those who reject Christ's claims? (2:14–16)

When we see Christians, ministers, and the gospel mocked and demeaned in films, television, and literature, how do Paul's words help us understand our secular society's hostility to the message of Christ? (2:16)

BIBLE EXTRA

In order to better understand 2 Corinthians 2:14, compare it with Romans 8:26–39, and answer the following questions. In the context of Romans 8:26–39, what does it mean that "all things work together for good to those who love God, to those who are called according to His purpose"? (Rom. 8:28)

Reflect on the context for both Romans 8:28 and 2 Corinthians 2:14, and write the way that they are similar.

How does praying in the Holy Spirit and intercession cause us to always triumph in Christ? (Rom. 8:26–27; 2 Cor. 2:14)

All ministers of the gospel who aim to be faithful, whether or not they are ever "flashy," at some point feel the force of the urgency of the gospel, of the need for lost humanity to hear and obey the gospel, and of the various natural, human, and demonic forces that hinder the effective spread of the gospel. They recognize how the ministry of the gospel requires, finally, supernatural empowerment, and they may cry out with the words that conclude 2:16. Write those here:

What is Paul's answer to this question? (2:17)

Our effectiveness in ministering to others is directly related to our integrity and sincerity. We must allow the Holy Spirit to purify our motives when we minister to others. Tragically, the Bible tells us that some people do not preach the gospel from pure motives. What is the unacceptable reason for which some preach? (2:17)

WORD WEALTH

Peddling referred, in Paul's time, to the work of small-time, unethical traders whom we would call hucksters today. Some of their dishonesty would include, for example, diluting good wine with water or using false weights in order to make an excessive profit on merchandise. Peddlers (from *kapēleuō*, Strong's *#2585*) were contrasted with legitimate merchants (from *emporos,* Strong's *#1713*).[2]

Although the vast majority of Christian ministers and ministries are working for Jesus Christ sincerely, some seem to have fallen into the trap of being concerned more with raising money than with ministering the life of Jesus to others. Even the most well-meaning religious enterprises can be subtly caught up in the pursuit of money, power, prestige, and influence, if they are not constantly holding themselves accountable and submitting themselves to the Lord Jesus Christ and to others in His body.

FAITH ALIVE

Spend a few minutes meditating on 2 Corinthians 2:17, and then prayerfully answer the following questions before the Lord. What motivates me to minister the gospel besides love for the Lord, the conviction that the gospel is God's only

way for saving men, and the conviction that He has called me
to ministry?

If I humbly acknowledge motives in addition to these,
which may be harmless byproducts of proper motives (such
as *enjoying* various tasks of ministry), and which are wrong
and harmful?

Which, if any, harmful motives are actively motivating
my ministry to any discernible degree now?

Is what I am teaching and preaching truly what God
wants said or am I trying to please men or earn position or
favor?

Am I *using* ministry—as opposed to offering ministry—in
any way for personal gain? (2:17)

To whom can I confess any sub-gospel motivation, so
that they can help me experience God's deliverance, walked
out a day at a time?

THE ORIGINAL LIVING BIBLE AND ITS MINISTERS (2 COR. 3:1–6)

After answering various criticisms against him, Paul
expresses some exasperation when he notices that he is beginning to "sell" himself—his qualifications as an apostolic minister—to the Corinthians. Why does Paul not need any letters of
recommendation to strengthen his relationship with the
Corinthians or to merit a higher estimation of worth from
them? (3:1–3)

Notice that in 3:2, 3, Paul turns the tables around:
Instead of needing any letters of recommendation, the

Corinthians themselves are such a letter—the proof that his ministry is genuine and effective. What three key agents are brought together in a close relationship? (3:3)

Who is the letter? (3:3)

The author? (3:3)

Who are the ministers? (3:3)

However certain Corinthians might wish to discredit Paul, what fact about Paul's role in their own existence as a church can they never deny? (3:3; also 11:2–3)

Imagine that you are one of the Corinthians who has been critical of Paul and would like to see other, more appealing leaders guiding the Corinthian church. What contrast between Paul's relationship to your church and the relationship of other later-coming leaders to your church would verse 3 force you to acknowledge?

Based on these verses, contrast Paul over against the "some" of verse 1, with these categories:

Categories for Contrast	Paul	"Some" of v. 1
What commends him/them as effective ministers of the gospel?		
How has each contributed to the birth and health of the Corinthian church?		

Despite Paul's evident accomplishment—the Corinthians themselves as an epistle of Christ—Paul's confidence in the carrying out of his ministry is placed in whom? (3:4)

The question he first asked in 2:16, Paul answers directly in 3:5 and 6. Write that answer here:

Implied in this answer is a rejection of other sources for the sufficiency of the minister, for example, the praise of others and one's natural skills and abilities. An important transition occurs in verse 6. The minister is sufficient, or competent, not simply through God in a general way. What, according to verse 6, has God enacted that makes the minister competent, or effective?

Fill in the key terms from the following verses to follow the beginning of Paul's contrast between the old and the new covenants, or agreements, through which God has worked with His people:

new covenant	**old covenant (implied)**
3:6 _____	of the letter
3:6 gives life	_____
3:3 written by _____	written with _____
3:3 written on _____	written on _____

 BIBLE EXTRA

Read these key passages from the old covenant, and next to the terms above, write the reference for each passage that has the same words or idea: Jeremiah 31:31–34; Ezekiel 11:19; 36:26; Exodus 31:18; Deuteronomy 9:10.

PROBING THE DEPTHS

True Authority in Spiritual Leadership (2 Cor. 3:1–6):
The work of God among the Corinthians was one of the evidences of the legitimacy and divine authority of Paul's ministry. Yet Paul had to defend his authority at Corinth because his leadership was being challenged by others who were trying to control the church. The difference between Paul and his rivals was that Paul's authority came from God. His credentials validating his claim to be a legitimate minister of Christ were the Corinthians themselves. Their lives gave evidence that they are a "letter of Christ" or a living letter of recommendation regarding his ministry. Unlike Paul's opponents, who were trying to promote themselves, Paul did not need some kind of formal letter of introduction and recommendation. The proof of his ministry was the changed lives of the Corinthians.

Denominational accreditation, ministerial credentials, and theological training can all have a place in ministry. But what is the final proof of our legitimacy in ministry? (3:1–6)

PROBING THE DEPTHS

Avoiding Smallness of Soul (2 Cor. 3:5–8): The truth of God's Word should always be ministered in love, especially when we are dealing with tough issues like sin, hell, judgment, repentance, apostasy, and God's call to holiness. These truths should be communicated in a spirit of love. This does not mean that we compromise God's Word. It simply means that we communicate it in love and compassion. In Ephesians 4:15, the apostle Paul writes, "but, speaking the truth in love, may grow up in all things into Him who is the head—Christ."

Paul warns us of the danger of communicating God's Word literally, but not in a life-giving or loving manner. Much harm has been done to the spread of the gospel of Jesus Christ by Christians who have communicated the truth of God's Word in anger, self-righteousness, judgmentalism, with condescension and divisiveness—by "smallness of soul." Our hearts should be enlarged by the Holy Spirit with a passionate love for others.

A SUPERIOR COVENANT PRODUCES A SUPERIOR MINISTRY (3:7–18)

Why does Paul shift from the topic of letters of recommendation to a contrast of old and new covenants? The most satisfying answer comes by seeing this section as further contrasting not just the two covenants, but two kinds of ministry. Paul's opponents appear to have held up Moses and the Law as keys to full Christian spirituality. Yet their allegiance to the old covenant does not seem to have included keeping the Sabbath, circumcision, or food laws. These practices were problems for Paul with the Galatian believers, but such practices are not mentioned in 2 Corinthians.

So we are left with less certainty than we would like to have regarding the precise identity, beliefs, and practices of Paul's opponents, to whom he refers first in 2 Corinthians 3:1 as the "some" who need and carry letters of recommendation as they travel in ministry. But it is plausible that Paul's opponents were, like him, Jewish Christians. They came to Corinth after Paul had established the church. Like Paul, these late-comer missionaries honored the old covenant as "holy and just and good" (Rom. 7:12), as the unerring revealer of sin. But unlike Paul, his opponents had more confidence in the ability of the old covenant to promote life in Christ, life in the Spirit. And because they used this difference between them and Paul to discredit his leadership among the Corinthians, in 2 Corinthians 3:7–18 Paul critiques their faulty, misplaced devotion to the old covenant. He also highlights the superiority of God's new covenant through Jesus Christ and of the ministry that serves this new covenant.

Whenever Paul says "us" or "we" in this passage, he is referring to ministers of the new covenant (see 3:6). His aim throughout the passage is to uphold the ministry of purely the new covenant, not the mixture of old and new covenant that his opponents practice. Because his opponents have made such inroads with at least an influential part of the Corinthian church, Paul has to convince those believers of two things:

1. That the new covenant is superior to the old;

2. And that, therefore, the ministry of the new covenant alone is sufficient and superior to the ministry of the old alone or to any mixture of the old and the new.

If Paul succeeds, then he can expect the Corinthians to recognize that, despite any dislike of his personal style, his ministry is authentic and deserving of the honor due the covenant he ministers. Correspondingly, the mixed new-plus-old-covenant ministry of his opponents is inferior, despite how much any Corinthians may prefer the personal style of such ministers. The true worth of a ministry is determined by worth of the covenant one ministers, not by personal preferences that make up ministerial style.[3]

Rather than enhancing the Christian life, the Mosaic covenant was a ministry of what? (3:7)

The ministry of the new covenant, in contrast, is accompanied by what two desirable realities? (3:8, 9)

How do the two covenants differ in the way in which each expresses God's glory? (3:7–11)

How can the old covenant express, at the same time, God's glory and death? (3:6–11; Rom. 7:8–23; Gal. 2:21; 3:2, 3, 10–14)

AT A GLANCE

Complete the following table to help you see the contrasts Paul draws between the old and new covenants so that his hearers will keep their confidence placed surely in the covenant that gives life.

CONTRASTING THE COVENANTS (3:7–18)

Item	Old Covenant	New Covenant
Key person	(v. 7)	(vv. 14, 16)
Described as "ministry of"	(vv. 7, 9)	(vv. 8, 9)
Degree and duration of glory	(vv. 7, 11)	(vv. 8, 9, 11, 12)
Relation of "the veil"	(v. 7)	(vv. 12, 14)
	(vv. 13–15)	(v. 18)
Role of the Spirit	(Spirit not related to the old covenant in 2 Cor. 3. Why do you think not?)	(vv. 8, 17, 18)
Final result of the glory imparted by each covenant	(vv. 13, 15)	(vv. 17, 18)

It is important to note that Paul does not belittle the old covenant, but that he exalts the new covenant. Based on your study of 2 Corinthians to this point, express in your own words how Paul would answer this question: "Why, Paul, is the new covenant so much better than the old?"

PROBING THE DEPTHS

Review the following passages of Scripture, and express for each how it appears to answer this question: What is the continuing role of the old covenant (and its law) in the Christian's life?

Matthew 5:17–20

Matthew 22:37–40

Romans 3:19–31

Romans 13:8–10

Galatians 5:1–6, 13–18

Drawing on all these passages, write answers to these questions:

How should the old covenant still influence the Christian (that is, in what way, if any, is it still binding)?

In what ways does the old covenant no longer influence the Christian?

If these seem like deep questions, you are not alone in feeling this way. Christians differ in their convictions about how the old covenant continues to be important for life under the new covenant, and these differences appear within the New Testament itself. For example, the differences in matters of conscience that Paul addresses in Romans 14 and 15 arise from how believers feel the force of old covenant commandments upon their lives in Christ. Rather than insisting that all the Christians agree on this doctrinal point, on what does Paul insist in the following verses from Romans 14?

v. 1

v. 3

v. 5

v. 13

v. 15

vv. 20, 21

     ## BIBLE EXTRA

"A Better Covenant"

While Paul contrasts the old and new covenants in the compact verses of 2 Corinthians 3:6–18, nearly all of the Book of Hebrews contrasts the two to show how much better the new covenant is and to urge believers not to waver in their confidence in this new and living way. For a quick overview, look up the following references and complete the table displaying the points at which the new covenant is superior to the old.

Passage	What from the New Covenant	Is Superior to	What from the Old Covenant
Heb. 1:5–14	Jesus		_____
Heb. 3:1–6	_____		_____

Heb. 4:1–11 _____   a rest never
                                           entered into

Heb. 7:14—8:6_____   _____

Heb. 9:7–12;
10:1–4, 22 _____   _____

Heb. 9:7–8,
15–17   _____   _____

📖 **BIBLE EXTRA**

According to 2 Corinthians 3:9–16, Moses wore a literal veil over his face to prevent the children of Israel from seeing the full manifestation of God's glory. Read the account in Exodus 34:29–35, and note that Moses removed this veil when he was in the presence of the Lord but put it back on when he went back to talk to the children of Israel. Paul gives two reasons for Moses' use of the veil: (1) to mute the radiance of the glory on his face so the people could look at him; and (2) to prevent their disappointment when the glory began to fade away. Then Paul transforms the literal veil into a spiritual symbol, and he moves it from the face of Moses to the hearts of those who know God only through Moses, even when One greater than Moses has come, namely Jesus Christ. To this day, when such physical children of Israel, modern Jews, read their Hebrew Bible and reject Christ, this veil mutes the full glory of God's Word. Because Jesus is the Living Word of God, only by accepting Him for who God says He is is the veil removed. But for those who do turn to the Lord, God's Spirit liberates them from a muted, vanishing glory and transmits to them the life-giving and life-transforming permanent glory of God that shines from the face of Jesus.

In what three ways does our worship of God and the accompanying release of His glory on our lives affect our ability to share our faith with others? (3:12, 17, 18)

1.

2.

3.

From 2 Corinthians 3:18 and other Scriptures (notably John 1:1–3, 14; Rom. 8:29) we may outline the distinct action of Father, Son, and Spirit in our relationship to the Triune God. Understanding verse 18 in this way can help us to cooperate more fully with the work of the Holy Spirit in transforming us more and more into Christlikeness. What does Paul say believers do in this process? (v. 18)

Who causes believers' transformation?

What is the goal, or the result, of this transformation?

The British theologian John Taylor has called the Holy Spirit the "Go-Between God" because of His ministry of communicating the gifts and graces of Jesus Christ to us. It is He who draws us to our risen Lord and who establishes and maintains intimate communion between us and Him. He is the "Communications Officer" in the Godhead. In the process of our responsive communication with our Lord (which is what "communion" is), the image of the Lord is transferred through the medium of the Holy Spirit onto us. This fully Trinitarian action may be expressed by comparing God's action on us with (the now nearly outdated process of) making a carbon copy: An author writes his thoughts on a sheet of paper. The carbon sheet lying underneath the original sheet transfers the message on the original onto another sheet.

To apply this comparison to the action of the Triune God, draw a line between each item in the left column and the agent it corresponds to in the right column:

Author	**Believers**
Original message written on sheet of paper	**The Holy Spirit**
Carbon paper transferring message	**The Son**
Message received onto second sheet	**The Father**

 FAITH ALIVE

Consider this comment on 2 Corinthians 3:18 from the *Spirit-Filled Life® Bible:* " 'Beholding as in a mirror' connotes 'reflecting' as well as 'looking into.' As we behold 'the glory of the Lord,' we are continually 'transformed into the same image' by 'the Spirit of the Lord.' We, then, with ever-increasing glory, reflect what we behold."[4] Ponder the last sentence of that note. What significance for corporate and personal worship can you see in it?

How can you "behold the Lord" more in your life?

What can you "behold" less in order that you might behold Him more?

Spend some time worshiping the Lord either privately or at church and do the following:

* Praise and worship the Lord and allow His presence to fill your heart and soul.

* Delight in His presence and thank Him specifically for things that He has done in your life.

* Be conscious of His presence and allow Him to speak to you.

* Give Him any burdens you may be carrying and place them in His hands.

* Let His glory fill you and allow His glory to minister to and through you.

* As you are experiencing His glory, *expect* that He will release you from any bondage, anxiety, oppression, or fear that may be in your life.

* Know that 2 Corinthians 3:18 is a present reality: "Where the Spirit of the Lord is, there is liberty."

When you spend time beholding the Lord, you will discover that you will be released in many different dimensions in your life.

---

1. *Spirit-Filled Life® Bible* (Nashville: Thomas Nelson, 1991), 1663, map of Asia and Greece Revisited.

2. W. E. Vine, Merrill Unger, William White, Jr., *Vine's Complete Expository Dictionary of Old and New Testament Words* (Nashville: Thomas Nelson, 1996), 130, "Corrupt."

3. Linda L. Belleville, *2 Corinthians: IVP New Testament Commentary Series* (Downers Grove: InterVarsity Press, 1996), 95–98; and Ben Witherington III, *Conflict and Community in Corinth: A Socio-Rhetorical Commentary on 1 and 2 Corinthians* (Grand Rapids: Eerdmans, 1995), 378–384.

4. *Spirit-Filled Life® Bible*, 1756, note to 2 Cor. 3:18.

Lesson 3/Common Instruments of Uncommon Power (2 Corinthians 4)

In his book *I Was Wrong* and during various media interviews, former television evangelist Jim Bakker told how he built a television empire, succumbed to various temptations, and ended up in disgrace and in prison. Both the book and the interviews provide mesmerizing accounts of personal moral and spiritual failure and of how God's redeeming hand reached out to a man whom much of the world had rejected and written off. Yet in the weakness of his being viewed by many as nothing but a "has been" con, Bakker witnessed powerfully to the reality of Christ's resurrection and to the infinite depths of God's love for each of us. The power of his witness did not rest in his eloquence and human ability to convince. In fact, it was a far different presentation of the gospel than he would have given in his "glory" days. Now, in his brokenness and humility, the reality of God's existence just seemed to pour through him. During his interview on CNN's "Larry King Live," God's handiwork was etched on the musculature of his face and expressed through the depth in his eyes and the faltering tone of his voice. It was a far cry from the arrogant style and emotionalistic manner he had used to build his earlier television empire.[1]

Yet in all the pain and suffering that accompanied God's stripping him of his fleshly self-reliance, this redeemed man of God was able to share in the most intimate manner the work of the risen Christ in his heart. It was such a stark contrast to the usual world of television, which seems to thrive on the superficial and sensationalistic. This evangelist had been crucified with Christ. In his weakness and death to self, he radiated the power of God with an authenticity that would give pause to even the most hardened cynic.

Paul presents himself and the gospel to the Corinthians in a manner like that of the humbled Bakker. But his opponents have made their inroads with the Corinthians at least in part because of their more pleasing style. Because people cling to their preferences of style tightly and emotionally, Paul does not respond to this issue directly at this point in the letter. Instead, he deals with more of a root issue, one that he can expect will be considered more thoughtfully and less emotionally. This issue is, What kind of ministry properly expresses the new covenant by conforming itself to the pattern of Jesus Himself?

MINISTERING THE LIFE OF JESUS IN A DARK WORLD (2 COR. 4:1–6)

Paul continues the theme of the glorious ministry of the glorious new covenant. What does he acknowledge as the reason he has "this ministry"? (4:1)

 WORD WEALTH

Mercy (*eleos* [*el*-eh-oss], Strong's *#1656*) means compassion, tender mercy, kindness, beneficence, and an outward manifestation of pity. The word is used of God (Luke 1:50, 54, 58; Rom. 15:9; Eph. 2:4); of Christ (Jude 21); and of men (Matt. 12:7; 23:23; Luke 10:37).

Mercy is the aspect of God's love that causes Him to help the needy or those in miserable, rejected, or unfortunate situations, just as grace is the aspect of His love that moves Him to forgive the guilty. Those who are miserable may be so either because of breaking God's law or because of circumstances beyond their control.

God shows mercy upon those who have broken His law (Dan. 9:9; 1 Tim. 1:13, 16). God's mercy on the needy or miserable extends beyond punishment that is withheld (Eph. 2:4–6). Withheld punishment keeps us from deserved judgment, but it does not necessarily grant blessing besides. God's mercy is greater than this.

God also shows mercy by actively helping those who are needy or in miserable straits due to circumstances beyond their control. We see this aspect of mercy especially in the life of our Lord Jesus. He healed blind men (Matt. 9:27–31; 20:29–34) and lepers (Luke 17:11–19). These acts of healing grew out of His commitment to reveal the will of God through acts of mercy.

Finally, because God is merciful, He expects His children to be merciful (Matt. 5:7; James 1:27).[2]

What effects on the minister does this glorious covenant have?

4:1

4:2

What are the "hidden things of shame" that Paul is talking about? (2 Cor. 4:2)

   WORD WEALTH

Shame is a negative emotion caused by an awareness of wrongdoing, hurt ego, or guilt. In the Bible, the feeling of shame is normally caused by public exposure of one's guilt (Gen. 2:25; 3:10). Shame may also be caused by a hurt reputation or embarrassment, whether or not this feeling is due to sin (Ps. 25:2–3; Prov. 19:26; Rom. 1:16).

Joseph, not wishing to shame Mary, desired to divorce her secretly (Matt. 1:19). Ultimately, God will expose the guilt of the ungodly, putting them to shame (Dan. 12:2). God also puts to shame the wise of the world by exposing their guilt before Him and by choosing to save the foolish of this world by a "foolish" message (1 Cor. 1:18–31). Finally, our Lord Jesus suffered the shame of the Cross because He was put on public display as the recipient of God's wrath (2 Cor. 5:21; Heb. 12:2).[3]

Exactly how do we renounce shameful things?

How do we make sure that we are not "handling the word of God" deceitfully? (4:2)

In 3:1–3, Paul refuses to commend his ministry (and team), yet in 4:2 he does. How does the way he will commend himself differ from the way he refuses to commend himself?

 WORD WEALTH

Craftiness (*panourgia,* Strong's *#3834*) means "versatile cleverness, astute knavery, sophisticated cunning, unscrupulous conduct, evil treachery, deceptive scheming, arrogant shrewdness, and sly arrogance. Used only five times in the New Testament, it refers to Satan's deceiving Eve (2 Cor. 11:3); the Pharisee's trying to trick Jesus (Luke 20:23); the deception of false teachers (Eph. 4:14); the self-entrapment of the worldly wise (1 Cor. 3:19); and the improper method of presenting the gospel (2 Cor. 4:2).[4]

"Craftiness" describes the kind of thinking and behavior that God does not want His people to adopt. This kind of wisdom is the "wisdom of the world" (1 Cor. 3:19), and it is not the wisdom that comes from God. All of us have known schemers and manipulators who attempt to engineer things for their own advantage, getting people to do things through trickery. Our society is permeated with that kind of thinking with certain politicians, salespeople, and advertisers, who deceive and manipulate others (knowingly or not) to accomplish their own goals. In many ways, our culture has lost its ability to discern truth from error. As a result, we often exalt image over substance. But this is not how God wants His people to behave. Christians are to be people of openness, accountability, and integrity in a dark world.

 PROBING THE DEPTHS

Christians and Culture: Identifying the Strongholds

A number of years ago there was a significant cultural shift in our society. It happened right after the "televangelist scandals" and the consequent fall of a number of prominent TV evangelists. What happened impacted the Christian culture at large, in that Satan secured a stronghold in the consciousness of our nation and world. Simply stated that stronghold was this lie: "Every Christian minister is dishonest, manipulative, only in it for the money, and probably sexually immoral."

While unethical ministers such as Sinclair Lewis's *Elmer Gantry* appeared from time to time in American literature and film the first half of this century, today's youths are exposed to almost nothing in the popular media besides stereotypes of Christian ministers portrayed as harshly judgmental, crooked, or bland and bumbling. The first way to deal with this false perception, or stronghold, in popular culture is for ordinary Christians and ministers to conduct themselves with integrity, intelligence, accountability, and transparency. The second way to deal with this stronghold is to fast and pray for our nation and ask God to tear down this stronghold erected by the enemy. (See 2 Cor. 10:1–5.)

 FAITH ALIVE

List four examples of how a Christian could make the mistake of "walking in craftiness," especially in ministry.

1.

2.

3.

4.

Now write down four ways a Christian can maintain integrity in life and ministry.

1.

2.

3.

4.

WORD WEALTH

Conscience (4:2) refers to a person's inner awareness of conforming to the will of God or departing from it, resulting in either a sense of approval or condemnation.

The term does not appear in the Old Testament but the concept does. David, for example, was smitten in his heart because of his lack of trust in the power of God (2 Sam. 24:10). But his guilt turned to joy when he sought the Lord's forgiveness (Psalm 32). Such passages as Psalm 19 indicate that God is discernible to the human conscience, and is accountable therefore (Rom. 1:18–20).

In the New Testament "conscience" is found most frequently in Paul's epistles. However, the conscience is by no means the final standard of moral goodness (1 Cor. 4:4). Under both the old and new covenant the conscience is trustworthy only when formed by the Word and will of God. The law given to Israel was inscribed on the hearts of believers (Heb. 8:10; 10:16), so the sensitized conscience is able to discern God's judgment against sin (Rom. 2:14–15).

The conscience of the believer has been cleansed by the work of Jesus Christ; it no longer accuses and condemns (Heb. 9:14; 10:22). Believers are to maintain pure consciences or not encourage others to act against their consciences. To act contrary to the urging of one's conscience is wrong, for actions that go against the conscience cannot arise out of faith (1 Cor. 8; 10:23–33).[5]

In 4:3 Paul may be responding to the criticism that his personal ministry is not impressive in terms of the numbers of converts it produces. How many vocational ministers and lay ministers fight discouragement because small numbers undermine their confidence in their ministries! Complete the following paraphrase of 4:2–7 to personalize Paul's message for ministers of the new covenant who may feel discouraged because their ministries do not appear to be as effective as they would want:

"As long as you are _____ (from 4:2),

then do not _____ (from 4:1). The smaller numbers you are

worrying about are due not to the quality of your ministry, but

to the fact that_____

_____ (from 4:3, 4). Continue to avoid the

temptation to_____ (from 4:5a); keep preaching

only _____ (from 4:5b)

and thinking of yourself as a _____ (from 4:5c).

Your job is to preach the new-covenant gospel honestly and

with integrity. Only God is able to _____

(from 4:6) into hearts darkened by the veil; you can't do that,

only _____(from 4:7) can."

What did Paul mean when he said "We do not preach ourselves, but Christ Jesus the Lord"? (4:5)

What would it mean for someone to "preach him- or herself"?

How can we make sure that we are magnifying Jesus Christ and not ourselves in our lives?

The classic chorus "Turn Your Eyes Upon Jesus" calls us to "look full in His wonderful face." Review and meditate on 3:18 and 4:6. Why is personal and corporate worship critical to our continuing to be transformed into Christlikeness?

How, according to this chorus and to 2 Corinthians 4, does a commitment to keep our eyes on Jesus and His humble glory help us resist the temptations that have sidetracked many believers, as they did Jim Bakker for a time?

MINISTERING THE LIFE OF JESUS THROUGH DAILY DISTRESSES (2 COR. 4:7–12)

Have you ever felt disqualified for spiritual service? Have you ever wondered if God really could ever use you? The apostle Paul understood those feelings, and that's why he wrote the words, "But we have this treasure in earthen vessels, that the excellence of the power may be of God and not of us" (2 Cor. 4:7). Sometimes when we look at people in public ministry, it's easy to get the wrong impression of what ministry is all about. In our media and television age, we often see so-called "celebrity Christians," "high-profile ministers" and big name evangelists who seem to have it all together. However, we don't get to see those people right after they just wake up in the morning or after a hard day's work or when the dishwasher breaks and the kids are screaming.

These people live in the same world you and I do. They have problems, faults, and shortcomings just like all of us. They do not walk around on some spiritual cloud going from victory to victory. The apostle Paul's words should hit home when he says, "we have this treasure in earthen vessels" (4:7). All of us are just ordinary people with human weaknesses and shortcomings. But the good news is that God can still use each one of us because effectiveness does not depend on us, but on the quality of the covenant we represent, so "that the excellence of the power may be of God and not us" (4:7).

God delights in taking ordinary people and doing something absolutely tremendous with their lives. A nationally known Bible teacher once told of the day when someone commented to her that, "God would never be able to use her because of her personality." At first the Bible teacher was insulted, but then she realized that it wasn't her personality that would make her successful anyway; rather Jesus, working through her and transforming her, would manifest His power.

This truth can free us from the bondage of trying to perform perfectly. Our job is not to be perfect (as a performer of ministry), but to trust in and cooperate with the Holy Spirit at work in and through us. As we walk with Him, He can take our ordinariness and manifest His extraordinary power.

What in 4:6 is "this treasure in earthen vessels" of 4:7?

"Earthen vessels" refers to the widespread use of clay for all kinds of household containers—jugs, pots, pans, and cups. The clay was common and unimpressive, fragile and easily broken. Yet people would regularly store valuables in them, just as God has placed His treasure in ministers of the new covenant who, like Paul, seem quite common and unimpressive to folks viewing things through the lenses of worldly values.

Paul extends this comparison of new covenant ministers with common "jars of clay" (NIV) through a list of unimpressive non-exploits in 4:8–12. List them:

v. 8a

v. 8b

v. 9a

v. 9b

v. 10a (symbolizing hardships just enumerated)

Express in your own words how Paul in verses 10 and 11 sees himself as following the pattern of Jesus, identifying daily with His death (see also 1 Cor. 15:31; Gal. 6:17):

Fill in the terms from 4:7 that correspond to these from 4:11b:
"the life of Jesus"   "manifested in our mortal flesh"

_____   _____

With this passage, you have reached a crucial point where you should now be able to express in a brief statement what Paul understands to be ministry in the Spirit and strength of Jesus. Review 4:7–15, and describe such ministry here:

What may such ministry lack so that critics may dismiss it as weak, unimpressive, and inadequate?

Based on 4:7–12, how would Paul answer the question, "How has God been at work in your ministry, showing it to be genuinely from him and Spirit-filled?"

Would that answer satisfy you? Why or why not?

MOTIVATION FOR MINISTRY AMID DAILY DISTRESSES (2 COR. 4:13–18)

In the midst of hardships such as those catalogued in 4:8–12, what motivated Paul to continue to speak the gospel boldly and not to "lose heart"? (4:13, 14; also 1 Cor. 15:14–19)

"All things" (4:15) refers to all that Paul and other faithful ministers of the new covenant have endured. How would Paul want verse 15 to relate to the criticisms leveled against him?

What does he want the Corinthians to see about his true motivation for ministry? (v. 15)

Despite the hardships that faithful new covenant ministry entails, what perspectives about ministry help Paul not to lose heart, according to verses 16–18?

Circle the following statement that best expresses this passage:

1. Our present afflictions while engaged in ministry will someday give way to eternal glory.

2. Our present afflictions in ministry will be done away with as soon as we exercise enough faith. Once they're gone, then we will experience the "eternal weight of glory" here and now.

3. Our present afflictions in ministry are producing an eternal weight of glory that we experience now, at least in part.

Experiencing eternal glory now requires what focus from us? (v. 18)

How does such a focus affect the way we look at the adversities we face in ministry?

From the choice offered in 4:18, what are those who are criticizing Paul looking at?

As a person involved in ministry, what does it mean for you not to look at the things that are seen and temporary?

What does it mean to look at the things that are not seen and eternal?

1. Jim Bakker, *I Was Wrong* (Nashville: Thomas Nelson Publishers, 1996).
2. *Spirit-Filled Life® Bible* (Nashville: Thomas Nelson Publishers, 1991), 1842, "Word Wealth: 2 Tim. 1:16, mercy"; *Nelson's New Illustrated Bible Dictionary*, Ronald F. Youngblood, Gen. Editor (Nashville: Thomas Nelson, 1995) "Mercy."
3. *NNIBD*, "Shame."
4. *Spirit-Filled Life® Bible*, 1723, "Word Wealth: 1 Cor. 3:19, craftiness."
5. *Hayford's Bible Handbook*, Jack W. Hayford, Gen. Ed. (Nashville: Thomas Nelson, 1995), 575, "Conscience."

Lesson 4/Truth, Accountability, and the Ministry of Reconciliation
(2 Corinthians 5)

We live in what the late theologian and philosopher Francis Schaeffer termed a "post-Christian culture." In fact, many analysts of contemporary society suggest that we now live in a "post-modern culture." In both a "post-Christian" and a "post-modern" culture, Christian virtues are often a thing of the past. Morality is now relative, ethics are situational, and thought has to be politically correct.

The fall-out from this kind of massive philosophical shift is cataclysmic. In a society which rejects the idea of right or wrong, anything goes. As such, we see college-educated students murder their newborn babies because the babies are an inconvenience. Drive-by shootings, white-collar crime, rape, and murder occur at an unprecedented rate. Our whole society seems to be in a kind of moral free fall.

Yet it is into this world that God has placed you and me to live as lights in the darkness. Our lives are to be like spiritual lighthouses for those who are lost in the sea of life. What makes our testimonies powerful is the fact that our Christian experience is rooted and grounded in truth, truth that has a factual historical record and corresponding contemporary experience. We aren't talking about some mystical "Jesus trip" or just some kind of religious experience not based in reality.

As Francis Schaeffer said, "Christianity is truth and not a religion." The Bible is not a collection of what author Joseph Campbell called myths to live by. The Bible is true in all that it teaches, whether regarding science, history, psychology, or theology. From these truths and teachings, the resurrection of Jesus Christ towers as supremely important.

In fact, the entire Christian experience is wrapped up in the resurrection of Jesus Christ. Men can have all kinds of intellectual arguments and philosophies which attempt to argue against the truth of the gospel of Jesus Christ. But if Jesus Christ rose from the dead, then all of these arguments come to nothing, because that which is universally agreed to be humanly impossible—to die and then come to life again, never to die again—has happened. The truth of the Resurrection is so important that the apostle Paul declared, "if Christ is not risen, then our preaching is empty and your faith is also empty" (1 Cor. 15:14).

The power and authority of the gospel stem from the fact that Jesus Christ really did rise from the dead in real space, time, and history. This occurrence of the Resurrection in regular time and space is what separates Jesus Christ from every other spiritual teacher, guru, and prophet throughout history. The Buddha, Muhammad, and all the other spiritual teachers are still dead. Only Jesus Christ rose from the dead as the unique Son of God (Rom. 1:4). And, as we see in 2 Corinthians 5, His resurrection gives us the confidence that God will not leave us at death either cold in the grave or as spirits without bodies.

THE REALITY OF THE RESURRECTION (2 COR. 5:1–8)

Chapter 5 continues the line of thought begun at 4:16. Review 4:16, and note the two reasons given in 4:17, 18 to support Paul's optimism. Both reasons begin with "for," and so does the third reason he gives in 5:1. What is that reason?

With 5:1 Paul tackles the topic of the believer's hope beyond the grave. What he says is important, although he does not say as much as we might wish. Let us put this new information in context: In chapter 4, Paul exalts the new covenant as the way God's power and permanent glory is expressed, both through ministers who are themselves fragile and common ("earthen vessels") and also through circumstances of sharp adversity. Chapter 4 concludes with the honest recognition that life in the new covenant is at once a death-in-progress ("our outward man is perishing") and the experience of continuous transformation from "glory to glory" (3:18; 4:18).

What happens to new covenant believers when they die? Paul's answer in 5:1–8 assures us that life continues beyond the grave, in God's presence.

How should we regard our present body in the light of the Resurrection? (5:1)

What desire does our belief in the Resurrection produce in us? (5:2–4)

In addition to the trustworthiness of God's Word, what kind of guarantee have we been given regarding the promise of our future destiny? (5:5)

BIBLE EXTRA

The cornerstone of the Christian faith is the bodily resurrection of Jesus Christ. The New Testament itself exists only because its several writers were absolutely sure that Jesus had risen. Most, if not all, of its writers were eyewitnesses of the risen Lord. Christ appeared after the Resurrection numerous times: The two followers in Emmaus encountered the resurrected Jesus and were so stunned that they forgot how late it was and rushed back to Jerusalem to tell the others (Luke 24:29–33). Thomas, who was the equivalent of a modern skeptic, wanted to be able to actually touch

Christ before he would believe. When Christ appeared to him and invited him to touch His wounds, Thomas's doubts melted into worship: "My Lord and my God!" he exclaimed (John 20:28).

Other followers of Jesus, such as Peter, encountered Him after His resurrection and left their fishing nets to enter the ministry (John 21:1–19). The apostle Paul was transformed into a missionary when the risen, ascended Jesus appeared to him (Acts 9:1–22). When Paul condensed the heart of Christian belief to a few affirmations (1 Cor. 15:1–7), he mentioned that over five hundred persons saw Christ after His resurrection. Many of those were yet alive when Paul wrote this passage of Scripture. As a result, our belief in the Resurrection rests on the testimony of a great number of people who had firsthand knowledge.

But our belief goes even beyond such historical eyewitnesses. In His final words to some of His followers before He ascended to heaven, Jesus told those historical eyewitnesses that they needed something else in order to be the kind of witnesses He wanted them to be: "He commanded them not to depart from Jerusalem, but to wait for the Promise of the Father," and He said, "But you shall receive power when the Holy Spirit has come upon you; and you shall be witnesses to Me in Jerusalem, and in all Judea and Samaria, and to the end of the earth" (Acts 1:4, 8).

God wants us to believe that Jesus rose again for two main reasons: (1) because we accept the sincere testimony of historical eyewitnesses who became effective spiritual witnesses by being filled with the Holy Spirit; and (2) by becoming witnesses ourselves of the fact that He is risen from the dead through experiencing the same outpouring of His Spirit, which is the Spirit of our ascended, exalted Lord (Acts 2:32–33). The outpoured Spirit makes unrepeatable, historical truth a contemporary, ongoing event in the lives of believers today.

What is the role of the Holy Spirit in assuring us that death is not final for believers? (5:5–6)

Of what are we confident, according to 5:6?

Based on 5:1–8, what does Paul teach about what happens to believers at death?

What is his attitude toward what happens to the believer at death? (5:6–8)

PERSONAL ACCOUNTABILITY BEFORE GOD (2 COR. 5:9–11)

You have probably heard the television commercial on investments in which the actor says, "We make money the old-fashioned way: we *earn* it." That may be true when it comes to making a return on a financial investment. But when it comes to salvation, the only way you can be saved is not through earning it. Rather, you receive salvation as a free gift from God through Jesus Christ.

The central message of the gospel is that we are saved entirely by faith and not through any kind of human effort. The Bible teaches us that there is absolutely nothing we can do to earn salvation. The apostle Paul said, "For by grace you have been saved through faith, and that not of yourselves; it is the gift of God" (Eph. 2:8).

Many people who call themselves evangelicals, fundamentalists, or charismatics believe that they are saved by faith. However, many who have experienced the joy of salvation are not clear what Scripture says about their accountability before God and what the Bible calls the "judgment seat of Christ" (2 Cor. 5:10).

 WORD WEALTH

Judgment seat, *bema,* in Matt. 27:19 and 2 Cor. 5:10. From *baino,* "to go," the word originally described a step or a stride (Acts 7:5). Then it was used for a raised platform reached by steps, especially from which orations were made. Later, it denoted the tribune or tribunal of a ruler where litigants stood trial. In the New Testament it usually refers to earthly magistrates (Acts 18:12, 16, 17), but twice it is used of the divine tribunal before which believers will stand (Rom. 14:10; 2 Cor. 5:10).[3]

What is the purpose of the *bema* in the believer's life? (5:10)

Paul states that every believer in Jesus Christ will stand before the judgment seat of Christ to "receive the things done in the body, according to what he has done, whether good or bad" (5:10). In other words, we are personally accountable before God for what we have done with our lives after we have been saved.

It is important that we do not misunderstand Scripture here. It's not that we are trying to sneak religious works back into the salvation picture. But the Bible does teach that all believers are directly accountable to God for what they have done with their time, talent, and abilities.

Many believers in Jesus Christ seem to think that after they have been saved, God has given them carte blanche with their lives. In other words, they think that after they have been saved they are free to live any way they choose as long as they don't sin. But this belief is not what the Bible teaches. We are responsible for faithfulness as parents, husbands, wives, children, employees, ministers, and citizens. God has invested many things into every one of our lives, and He expects us to be fruitful for His kingdom.

 BIBLE EXTRA

The accountability of believers appears numerous times in the New Testament. Look up the following references, and list ways you will be held accountable for your work in this life:

Matthew 25:14–46

Luke 19:12–27

John 5:25–27

Acts 10:42

In your own words, briefly explain how we can be saved by grace and yet still be accountable before God for our lives.

How can we take our accountability seriously but not become legalistic?

Based on what you have learned from 2 Corinthians and the other passages you have looked up, what do you think is the relationship between the "judgment seat of Christ" in 2 Corinthians 5:10 and the "great white throne of judgment" in Revelation 20:11?

Will any rewards be given to believers at the judgment seat of Christ? (James 1:12)

If individual Christians are faithful to what God has called them to do, what should be their attitude toward the judgment seat of Christ? (5:9–11, also 5:1–8)

What will believers who have lived their lives selfishly and disobediently experience at the judgment seat of Christ?

How does the blood of Jesus Christ affect what will happen at the judgment seat of Christ?

FAITH ALIVE

In what ways has your study of 2 Corinthians 5 caused you to understand your personal accountability differently?

Spend a few moments worshiping the Lord and thanking Him for His grace in your life. Meditate on the fact that God totally accepts you as you are and that there is absolutely nothing you can do to earn His love, favor, or acceptance. Ask God in prayer if there is any area in your life which needs change. Allow the Holy Spirit to speak to you about your faithfulness as a husband, wife, father, mother, child, student, parent, employee, citizen, or minister. Then write down the areas about which God has spoken to you. Develop a clear, simple, and concise action plan to begin living more accountably.

Areas about which God Has Spoken to Me	Action Plan for Change

Whether alive on earth or alive beyond the grave, what should be the aim of every believer? (5:9)

What form of accountability does Paul teach awaits all believers? (5:10)

THE MINISTRY OF RECONCILIATION (2 COR. 5:12–21)

In 2 Corinthians, Paul reached out to the Corinthians to reestablish an intimate relationship. Paul had experienced a close, eighteen-month relationship with them and was baring his heart to them. He was not coming down to them from some tower of ecclesiastical authority. He regarded them as coworkers in the ministry of reconciliation. Yet Paul understood that if they were not fully reconciled to him as Christ's representative, then they could not fully be reconcilers to others. Certain things and people stood in the way of this reconciliation. Competitors, whom Paul called "false apostles," were trying to win the hearts of the young Corinthian converts. Paul's statement to the Corinthians was "that God was in Christ reconciling the world to Himself, not imputing their trespasses to them, and has committed to us the word of reconciliation" (2 Cor. 5:19). The very heart of the gospel is reaching out to reconcile others to God—not condemning them or attacking them, but winning them in love.

What do Paul's words in 2 Corinthians 5:18–20 tell us about his attitude toward the church?

What can we learn from Paul's perspective in dealing with the church? (5:12–21)

How does 2 Corinthians 5:20 reveal Paul's passion for the church?

How should our status as "ambassadors for Christ" affect the way we proclaim the gospel to those who are involved in "sinful lifestyles" and appear to be antagonistic to the things of God? (5:20)

WORD WEALTH

"reconciled," *katallasso* means "to change, exchange, reestablish, restore relationships, make things right, remove an enmity. Five times the word refers to God's reconciling us to Himself through the life, death and resurrection of His Son Jesus (Rom. 5:10; 2 Cor. 5:18). Whether speaking of God and man or husband and wife, *katallasso* describes the reestablishing of a proper, loving relationship, which has been broken or disrupted."[1]

In examining the word reconciled, we gain a rich understanding of what real ministry is all about. In your own words, explain how the following terms relate to the quality of ministry that Jesus Christ wants us to have.

Change

Reestablish relationships

Restore relationships

Make things right

Remove enmity

CHRIST'S LOVE IS THE ONLY MOTIVE FOR MINISTRY (2 COR. 5:12–15)

Paul found himself in the awkward position of having to defend the legitimacy of his ministry to some of the Corinthians. As immature Christians, they were evaluating Paul on the basis of worldly and superficial criteria. In verse 14, Paul reveals the heartbeat of all genuine and authentic ministry.

What seems to be Paul's motivation for ministry? (5:14)

Paul writes, "for the love of Christ compels us." Paul had allowed the Holy Spirit to purify his inner motives for ministry. He was gripped and consumed by the love of Christ for others. He wasn't trying to build a ministerial career, attempting to authenticate himself, or trying to establish himself. His heart was on fire and consumed with a passionate love for Jesus Christ which sought to help others.

What was the difference between Paul's motives and those of his competitors? (5:12)

How important are our true motivations in ministry?

If our motivations are not pure in ministry, in what ways might we expect God to deal with us as a loving heavenly father?

THE CORINTHIANS' IMAGE OF CHRISTIAN LEADERSHIP (2 COR. 5:16–17)

One of Paul's goals as a spiritual leader was to try to mature the Corinthians' perspective on how to evaluate leadership. The Corinthians had some very worldly notions about what it takes to be a Christian leader. It seems that they formed their opinions about a Christian leader based on an earthly perspective and using worldly standards of judgment. Ben Witherington III writes in *Conflict and Community in Corinth,*

> In short, the fundamental problem is the Corinthians' image of Christian leadership. At least some of them had created in their minds an image, largely shaped by the values of the culture, of a leader who had honor, power, spiritual gifts, rhetorical skills, good references and who would accept patronage. They looked, that is, for a Sophist, or at least a rhetorically adept philosophical teacher."[2]

In short, the Corinthians judged the worth of a Christian leader based on the values of the surrounding culture and not on biblical ones.

Before Paul became a believer in Jesus, he evaluated Him "according to the flesh." What was his evaluation of Jesus? (Acts 9:1–4)

What would it mean to evaluate a Christian leader "according to the flesh" today?

What happens to the effectiveness of the church if it uses worldly notions of leadership and power in calling, training, and ordaining its leaders?

How does 2 Corinthians 5:17 change the way we look at ourselves and others?

How does 2 Corinthians 5:16–17 help clarify what leadership patterned after Jesus looks like today?

How does 2 Corinthians 5:16–17 help Christian leaders and followers work in harmony with the principles of life that are part of the "new creation"?

Thinking of what you have learned from your study of 2 Corinthians to this point, how did the life and ministry of Jesus Christ model true spiritual leadership?

How was Paul's leadership modeled after Jesus Christ's?

1. *Spirit-Filled Life® Bible* (Nashville: Thomas Nelson Publishers, 1991), 1728, "Word Wealth: 1 Cor. 7:11, reconciled."

2. Ben Witherington III, *Conflict and Community in Corinth* (Grand Rapids: Eerdmans, 1995), 348.

Lesson 5/Ministering Jesus in the Real World
(2 Corinthians 6—9)

How does society at large perceive Christian ministers today? Sadly, an unbelieving world often has a very cynical and jaundiced view of those in ministry. This cynicism is especially heightened among those of the younger generation, who often see Christian ministers as opportunists, fanatics, and money seekers.

Hollywood has contributed to this misconception by its endless films and television specials about corrupt evangelists and psychopathic Christians. To compound the problem, the television evangelist scandals over the past decade significantly added to the negative image that the motion picture and television industry created. Elmer Gantry-style evangelists are a favorite staple of screenwriters and film producers. We concede, sadly, that some have presented themselves as legitimate ministers of the gospel, only to be shown to have manipulated and cheated people looking to them for hope in desperate circumstances.

This culture of cynicism and mockery of Christian ministers and evangelists has become part of the fabric of life. It is quite common to hear people say, "Be healed!" and slap somebody on the forehead as a joke these days.

It's in this context of cynicism and doubt that today's ministers and evangelists are called to preach the gospel. Although the apostle Paul did not have to deal with mass media, he did have to deal with the cynicism of a popular culture and those who accused him of being a phony. In 2 Corinthians, we learn how Paul's integrity and character were attacked and how he responded by calling believers to evaluate him in light of the gospel and example of Jesus. Those set the standard to which we must continue to conform our life and ministry.

PREACHING THE MESSAGE OF SALVATION IN A REAL WORLD (2 COR. 6:1–10)

The apostle Paul had a burning desire to preach the message of salvation to a lost and dying world. However, he knew that his effectiveness as a minister and a Christian was directly related to his personal integrity. Integrity produces spiritual power in ministry. In addition, Paul was attempting to prove to some of the Corinthians why his ministry was an authentic and legitimate ministry. In preaching the gospel, Paul did not want his words to have a hollow echo. First of all, Paul sought to be diligently beyond reproach (6:3). Second, Paul wanted the Corinthians to know that there was a price to be paid for excellence in ministry. Paul personally endured great hardship and suffering in order to be able to preach the gospel.

Read 2 Corinthians 6:4–5, and list the nine things Paul had to endure and which he used to commend his ministry to the Corinthians.

1.   6.

2.   7.

3.   8.

4.   9.

5.

A MODEL FOR MINISTRY (2 COR. 6:3)

The words of the apostle Paul should echo in the hearts of all those today who wish to go into a ministry of any kind. He said, "We give no offense in anything, that our ministry should not be blamed" (6:3). In every aspect of his life and ministry, Paul was fully conscious of the fact that he was an ambassador for Christ (2 Cor. 5:20). Even though his critics attempted to attack him personally and discredit his ministry, Paul lived a life that was above reproach (2 Cor. 4:2). Yet, as we have seen and will see, some Corinthians and other unnamed leaders hailing from Jerusalem attacked just these things—Paul's character and integrity. Because we leaders today often experience the same unjustified attacks because of society's cynicism, we can learn from Paul a truly Christlike way to respond to such attacks.

Why is it important as ministers of the gospel that "we give no offense in anything"? (6:3)

How can a lack of integrity in our ministry and personal life give Satan a foothold in launching an attack against us?

Why is being above reproach in our life more important than the words we speak?

BUILDING *KOINONIA*—THE CHRISTIAN LEADER'S GOAL (2 COR. 6:11—7:1)

One of the apostle Paul's strategies in maturing the church at Corinth was to further develop *koinonia* (partnership). The obstacles to building *koinonia* were the influence of false apostles, partnership in pagan worship and rituals, and associations with nonbelievers (6:15). Paul understood that as long as these young converts continued to be influenced by nonbelievers, the believers were going to be inhibited in their spiritual growth. Paul was trying to bind the Corinthians more closely to him and to each other so that true Christian fellowship could be created.

Why did Paul not want the Corinthians to be "unequally yoked together with unbelievers"? (6:14)

BIBLE EXTRA

Look up the following references from 1 Corinthians and list the kind of "unequal yoking" each responds to:

5:1–13

6:1–6

6:12–20

10:6–22

What negative result can occur if partnership or fellowship continues between "light and darkness"? (2 Cor. 6:14)

What practical spiritual result happens when unhealthy fellowship is broken? (6:16–18)

WORD WEALTH

Fellowship (2 Cor. 6:14): Paul asks the question, "For what fellowship has righteousness with lawlessness?" (6:14). The word fellowship *(koinonia)* means "sharing, unity, close association, partnership, participation, a society, a communion, a fellowship, . . . help, the brotherhood."[1] For Christians, fellowship with darkness or pagan practices is spiritually destructive. Yet, in the positive sense, *koinonia* is a unity brought about by the Holy Spirit. "In *koinonia* the individual shares in common an intimate bond of fellowship with the rest of Christian society. *Koinonia* cements the believers to the Lord Jesus Christ and to each other."[2]

What does understanding the term fellowship or *koinonia* teach us about the power of our relationships?

What role does a Christian leader have in helping to develop *koinonia*? (6:11, 12)

What do you think fellowship provides that is essential to maturing the church, along with prayer and Bible study?

 BEHIND THE SCENES

Some of the Corinthians, especially some of the more affluent Gentiles, were attending feasts in pagan temples or dining rooms that were connected to temples (1 Cor. 8—10). These dinners often involved pagan ceremonies and an animal sacrifice dedicated to a pagan deity. Paul warned that participation in any kind of pagan worship was idolatry. One of these pagan temples was the Asklepion, where pagan banquets occurred. Paul warned believers that they could not partake at the table of demons and the table of the Lord at the same time (1 Cor. 10:21–22). Although in contemporary society we do not have specifically pagan banquets where animals are sacrificed, we do have cultural activities which would be the modern equivalent of pagan feasts in that these activities make place for demonic activity and idolatry. Certain nightclubs, movies, theatrical productions, parties, and social occasions open the door to demonic bondage. Certainly not all nonreligious social events fit into this category. But the warnings of the apostle Paul apply to modern believers, and in these days of increasing demonic influence in the culture at large, we must discern which activities and relationships are good for people committed to following the Holy Spirit to use for recreation and leisure and which should be avoided.

What kinds of films, social events, parties and celebrations would amount to the modern equivalent of pagan worship?

How can a believer discern whether the above events would be spiritually safe or not?

BIBLE EXTRA

You Are the Temple of the Living God
(2 Cor. 6:14—7:1)
Paul calls the believers in Corinth to holy living. He begins by warning them not to be "unequally yoked together with unbelievers" (v.14). The concept comes from Leviticus 19:19 which prohibits yoking different types of animals together. Not only is Paul referring to marriage partnerships as in 1 Corinthians 7:39, where he warns believers not to marry unbelievers, but Paul is referring to any intimate partnership with nonbelievers. The reason for this? "What communion has light with darkness? And what accord has Christ with Belial?" (6:14–15). The name *Belial* can be translated "the chief of demons, or Satan." Finally, Paul teaches us that as believers we are "the temple of the living God" (6:16).

When believers allow the idolatry of the world to enter into their hearts, they are opening the door for demonic influence and bondage. God wants believers to be cleansed from all "filthiness of the flesh and spirit" (7:1) because He wants to set them free and make their lives and ministries fruitful. Holiness produces freedom and releases spiritual power in the lives of believers.

In what ways can a believer enter into a wrong partnership with the world? (6:14)

Identify the kinds of things which could be called idolatry in the life of a believer. (6:16)

How can we as believers "cleanse ourselves from all filthiness of the flesh and spirit" and "perfect holiness"? (7:1)

Why is holiness important for Christians? (7:1)

What is the relationship between holiness and the release of spiritual power? (6:16—7:1)

THE TENDERNESS OF TOUGH LOVE (2 COR. 7:2–16)

What parents have not disciplined children, found the process necessary but painful to themselves, and looked forward to the moment when they could hug their children and pour on the affection? That scene illuminates these verses (review 6:11–13).

Paul sounds like a parent at what stage of the correction-reconciliation process in 7:2–4?

Read 7:5–6, and find Macedonia (where Paul was when he wrote 2 Corinthians) on the map in lesson 2, and identify the likely route Titus followed from Corinth to visit Paul.

Verse 4 mentions "all our tribulation." Reread the following passages to review what Paul has written earlier in this letter about his tribulations: 1:3–11; 4:8–11; 6:3–10.

What was the purpose of the "epistle [that] made you sorry"? (7:8–12)

    PROBING THE DEPTHS

What was the "severe letter," and what was the problem it aimed to correct?

This letter is referred to in 7:8–12 and earlier in 2:3–11. It was "written as a follow-up to the *painful visit.* Some identify 1 Corinthians as the *severe letter,* but it does not seem to fit that description. Others suggest that 2 Corinthians 10—13 fits that description, but no manuscript evidence supports the separation of those chapters from the rest of the epistle."[3] The problem that letter aimed to correct "involved a challenge to Paul's authority as an apostle. The *severe letter* achieved a degree of correction. The rebel who 'caused grief,' not merely for Paul, but for the entire church 'to some extent,' had been repudiated 'by the majority' (see 7:6–13). With their cooperation, Paul is ready 'to forgive and comfort' the offender. To continue to punish him (after he has repented) would damage not only him but the church and Paul's own work, because it would allow 'Satan' to 'take advantage' of the discord in the church. The traditional identification of the offending person with the incestuous man in 1 Corinthians 5:1–5 is possible, but the offense here seems to have been directed particularly at Paul with the charge being grievous, rude conduct, not immorality."[4]

What news did Titus bring Paul, and what was the effect of that news on the apostle? (7:6–7)

Paul commends the Corinthians for one action and for the manner in which they acted. Write both here. (7:8–11)

Like a good parent, Paul makes clear his aim in sending the letter of correction. What aim does he want the Corinthians to notice and accept? (7:12)

Identify the sources and receivers of comfort in 7:13–16.

Review all of chapter 7, and list the things Paul rejoices about:

What do you think Paul is trying to accomplish throughout chapter 7 by commending the Corinthians, by telling them how he rejoices in them, and by describing his actions toward them as meant for their good?

MINISTRY AND MONEY (2 COR. 8:1—9:15)

Faithfulness and stewardship regarding money is an essential part of all ministry and an extremely important aspect of Christians' lives. The apostle Paul tells us in 1 Timothy 2:10, "For the love of money is a root of all kinds of evil." Notice that Paul does not say money is evil, but it is the "love of money" which is evil. In 1 Timothy 3:3 and in Titus 1:7, Christian leaders are warned not to be greedy for money. Jack Hayford relates the story of a prominent minister who called him in order to be accountable to him in ministry. One of the questions Dr. Hayford asked him was, "How much is your salary?" Dr. Hayford went on to say that a minister of the gospel should receive a fair remuneration for his work but that it should not be excessive. God does not want ministers to be poor and needy; but neither are they supposed to get rich from the ministry.

 FAITH ALIVE

In 1 Corinthians 6:12 the apostle Paul writes, "All things are lawful for me, but all things are not helpful. All things are lawful for me, but I will not be brought under the power of any." As ambassadors of Jesus Christ, the things that we do no longer represent us, but the one we represent, who is the Lord Jesus Christ. Therefore, we should exercise wisdom regarding the clothes we wear, the cars we drive, the homes in which we live, the words we use, and the general conduct of our lives. People are watching Christians and ministers of the gospel to see if our conduct fits that of our Master and Lord.

This does not mean that we cannot have nice clothes, cars, homes, or enjoy life—all of these as gifts of a generous

God. But it does mean that we will be held accountable for the choices we make. We must prayerfully consider how other people may perceive our choices and styles and be drawn to, or repelled from, our verbal witness to the gospel.

 ## FAITH ALIVE

Spend some time in prayer and ask God to reveal to you anything that may be a stumbling block to others. The Lord may tell you to change some things in your life. Perhaps He may ask you to do something entirely unexpected. Rather than being ostentatious, a person may be making the opposite mistake. Is it possible that you are causing people to stumble by not dressing sharply enough, not having an acceptable car, or not maintaining a decent home? Remember, as an ambassador, everything you do represents the "kingdom" you are serving.

Write down the things the Lord is speaking to you. Then ask yourself the following questions.

- Does the way I dress properly represent the ministry to which God has called me?

- Does the car I drive and the way I maintain it represent the kingdom of God?

- What changes in my lifestyle is God asking me to make?

What does the giving of the Macedonian churches teach us about the proper attitude in giving? (8:1—9:15)

How can one who thinks himself to be poor also be a generous giver in God's eyes? (8:1–4)

What does the giving of the widow, along with the comments of Jesus, teach about the kind of giving God blesses? (Luke 21:1–4)

What is the grace God bestowed on the Macedonian churches? (2 Cor. 8:1–3)

In what way is liberality in giving a manifestation of God's grace? (also Rom. 12:4–8)

What were the collected funds to be used for? (2 Cor. 8:4)

BEHIND THE SCENES

We derive general teaching about giving from Paul's direction to the Corinthians about the collection he was taking up from predominantly Gentile churches in Macedonia and Achaia (see map in lesson 2; also Rom. 15:26) for the poorer Jewish believers in Judea. These Jewish Christians had been severely affected by the famine which occurred during the reign of the emperor Claudius (A.D. 41–54). The offering being taken up among Paul's churches was intended as aid to all these believers in need, and it would have gone mainly toward purchasing food.

Paul wants the Corinthians to experience what manifestation of God's grace? (8:1, 6–7)

Why did Paul send Titus to the Corinthians? (8:6–7)

Paul does not command the Corinthians to give. By citing the example of the Macedonian believers, as well as the example of Jesus, how is Paul hoping to motivate them to complete the act of giving they had already started? (8:7–9)

WORD WEALTH

"Became poor" in 8:9 comes from *ptocheuo,* which means "To be destitute, poor as a beggar, reduced to extreme poverty. The word suggests the bottom rung of poverty, a situation in which one is totally lacking in this world's goods."[5]

BEHIND THE SCENES

In 2 Corinthians 8:9 we are told that Jesus "became poor." What exactly His poverty consisted of is debated. Was it His leaving the riches of glory and, in the language of Philippians 2:8–9, "being found in appearance as a man, He humbled Himself and became obedient to the point of death, even the death of the cross"? Or was His poverty material—being born into a poor family and living among those of lower social classes? One does not exclude the other. Materially, Jesus was not among the poorest of the poor. His father worked a trade, carpentry, which Jesus learned; and during His ministry, Jesus had the financial support of a number of well-off followers who had been healed and touched by Him. Whatever "His poverty" denotes exactly, Paul's point is that Jesus voluntarily gave up His rightful claim to being honored and served by others and became the servant of others, making them rich through His poverty.

Review these Scriptures, and list the riches each mentions which the Corinthians received through Christ's poverty:

1:22; 5:5

4:16

4:18

5:1

5:8

5:17

5:18

5:21

What is Paul's advice regarding the Corinthians' giving? (8:10–12)

What goal for the giving of the churches does Paul express in verses 13–15?

What shows Titus's "earnest care" for the Corinthians? (8:6, 16)

If, as seems the case, some at Corinth suspected that Paul was in some way misusing the offering intended for the Judean saints, what is said in verses 17–24 to disarm that suspicion?

Paul adds to the force of his appeal by informing the Corinthians about what he has told the Macedonians about them. What had he told? (9:1–2)

What reason does Paul give for sending "the brethren" to the Corinthians? (9:3–5)

What result of their being unprepared do these verses imply that Paul wishes to spare the Corinthians and himself (!), were the Macedonian Christians to visit? (9:4–6)

Read 9:6–10, and for each topic listed below, write out what you believe is the main point from that passage.

Sowing and reaping (v. 6)

Cheerful giving (v. 7)

The source of abundance (v. 8)

How giving is multiplied (v. 10)

Two results of generous giving (v. 12)

Two actions the recipients of the gift will perform (v. 13, 14)

What would the Corinthians' generous giving demonstrate at work in them? (9:14; compare with 8:1)

In this passage, Paul teaches that God multiplies the resources of the believer who gives generously. But this abundance is tied to God's own purpose—"for all liberality"—that is, in order to be generous in all circumstances. Material blessing or extra income in and of themselves are not set up as signs of God's blessing, nor is the specific act of giving itself praised. Instead, Paul commends "a lifestyle of generosity. . . . Those who give cheerfully and willingly" are promised "that God will provide all that they need to continue doing good."[6]

FAITH ALIVE

In the world system of economics, the fear of not having enough is a prime motivator. This fear of poverty and lack creates a climate of economic manipulation, the hoarding of resources, the love of money, dishonest and unethical business dealings, and many other social ills. The Christian's relationship to money should never be one of fear. A Christian should see God as the source of all money and resources. A Christian's mind should be renewed by the Word of God, which defeats a "poverty" or "lack" mentality.

Instead of fear, the Christian should have faith in God's ability to provide and His demonstrated willingness to replenish the resources of those who give properly—generously and regularly for the good of others and the glory of God. Paul wrote to some of those poor but generous Macedonian Christians, the Philippians, "My God shall supply all your need according to His riches in glory by Christ Jesus" (Phil. 4:19). That affirmation applies only to those who participate in God's economy in the way that Paul encouraged the Corinthians to participate.

Unlike the world's system of economics, God's system is wrapped up in the principle of giving generously and regularly. In addition, God has established the law of sowing and reaping. In giving in order to bless others, we discover that we are blessed.

Instead of trying to hold on to, persevere, and get more for ourselves, God has given us the privilege of sowing seed into the lives of others. This seed may take the form of love, time, prayer, or money. As we seek to give generously toward the needs of others, then God takes care of our needs. This truth is central to all ministry that is effective and offered in the spirit and strength of Jesus.

Take a moment to review what God is saying to us in 2 Corinthians 8—9. Then write below what single understanding or direction for your life stands out to you the most.

What action does that insight or direction invite you to take this week?

1. *Spirit-Filled Life® Bible* (Nashville: Thomas Nelson Publishers, 1991), 1628, "Word Wealth: Acts 2:42, fellowship."

2. Ibid.

3. Ibid., 1753, note on 2 Cor. 2:3, 4.

4. Ibid., 1754, note on 2 Cor. 2:5–11.

5. Ibid., 1761, "Word Wealth: 2 Corinthians 8:9, became poor."

6. Linda L. Belleville, *2 Corinthians: IVP New Testament Commentary Series* (Downers Grove: InterVarsity Press, 1996), 241.

Lesson 6/Overcoming Challenges in Christian Leadership
(2 Corinthians 10—11:15)

Farmer Bill couldn't catch the mouse that kept helping himself to the grain for the feeder calves. Traps didn't work, neither did poison, nor two scrawny cats. The thought of being beaten by the puny mouse so possessed Farmer Bill that he took up a 'round-the-clock vigil in the barn, armed with his prized double-barrel shotgun.

The crafty mouse kept a low profile, but finally hunger pushed him from hiding, along the edge of the loft, toward the bags of grain. Farmer Bill awoke from a doze with a start, and in a single fluid motion grabbed the shotgun, leveled it, and fired—just as the mouse scampered in front of a box of dynamite.

Farmer Bill's obituary noted that he got the mouse.

Life is filled with conflict. We choose how to respond and, by our responses, show if we want the conflict to heat up or to cool down, to continue or to be resolved. Because we are only part of the conflict, we often cannot control the outcome, only our response. At times it is hard to know how to respond. How can we be truthful and loving and act in a way that also has the potential of being effective?

In his stormy relationship with the Corinthians, Paul faced the greatest church conflict of his ministry (at least that we know about from his New Testament letters). As we have seen in previous lessons of this guide, Paul's motives and actions were questioned by opposing leaders who wanted pride of place among the Corinthian church, as well as by at least some (but not all; see 7:6–16) of the Corinthian believers themselves.

What would you do when such questioning, open criticism, and calls for your replacement—all in your absence— jangle in your ears, and you are still out of the country? What would you do when you are convinced that it is not only you who is being rejected, but the pure gospel itself? When a proper understanding of Jesus is replaced with another Jesus, a Jesus who merely reinforces the dominant values of the local culture, and does so by eliminating dimensions of the biblical Jesus that are not attractive to a proud, self-willed culture?

Chapters 10—13 merit close study by all leaders, because all leaders will face opposition and conflict. And Paul's response, studied patiently, is a worthy case study of a servant-leader who struggled against worldliness in the hearts of the yet-carnal Corinthians and who sought to call them—at times tenderly, at times sternly—back to the humble Christ who is powerful through what looks like weakness to a worldly mind-set. Paul sought to resolve this serious conflict with spiritual firepower that would destroy spiritual opposition without destroying the resistant Corinthians, whom he loved like a father. It is a case study that shows us what it means to minister in the Spirit and strength of Jesus while under fire.

LOVE THAT FIGHTS (2 COR. 10:1–11)

Read 2 Corinthians 10:1–11 several times aloud. Experiment by reading verses with different interpretations coming through your voice. Paul is exasperated at this point in the letter, having taken the long, indirect route to deal with the main problem. He used the indirect approach to help the Corinthians focus on their partnership with him in Christ. Now he deals with the core issue—the move to deny him any more leadership influence in the congregation. So some of the words in chapters 10—13 should sound pained, some even sarcastic, some urgently appealing. After reading 10:1–11 several times, answer these questions:

With what tone, or manner of approach, does Paul want to deal with the Corinthians and this conflict? (10:1)

How has Paul been "lowly" in person, but "bold" from a distance? (10:1–2, 8–11)

What is the difference between walking "according to the flesh" (with which Paul's critics charge him) and walking "in the flesh" (which Paul acknowledges that he—and every person—does)? (10:2–4; see the similar contrast between "in the world" and "not of the world" in John 15:19; 17:11).

Paul claims that he does not walk "according to the flesh" because he does not "war according to the flesh." What does verse 4 say that clarifies what warring "according to the flesh" would be?

Instead of warring "according to the flesh," how—with what—does Paul fight? (10:3–4)

At what four targets do Paul's weapons "mighty in God for pulling down strongholds" aim? (10:5–6)

(v. 5a) cast down_____

(v. 5b) cast down _____

(v. 5c) bring_____

(v. 6a) be ready to_____

Verse 5c may be paraphrased: "arresting every thought and making it obedient to Christ." Keeping in mind the terms that here point to thoughts and opinions ("strongholds," "arguments," "knowledge," "thought"), by reading 10:7–17 as a unit, write here the opinion, or perspective, held by Paul's critics that he is opposing with spiritual weapons.

How high-quality will any evaluation be that focuses only on "outward appearance"? (10:7)

What is the major complaint against Paul? (10:7–8)

For what purpose is spiritual authority given by God? (10:8)

What do his critics complain about concerning Paul's public presentation? (10:10)

What do you think of someone who is mousy in person but a "big talker" when he's away from the people he is challenging?

A MINISTRY BEYOND COMPARISON (2 COR. 10:12—11:15)

Review lesson 1. Based on your study so far, list the criticisms you think Paul's opponents compiled against him. (10:1–18)

In what ways is Paul's ministry different from those of the opposing leaders? (10:12–18)

Paul's opponents have evaluated themselves positively, but the apostle quite negatively. Why is their self-evaluation flawed? (10:12)

What special relationship with the Corinthians does Paul point to that the opposing leaders do not and can never have with these believers? (10:13–14)

How does that special relationship give Paul authority in the Lord that includes the Corinthians? (10:13–15)

"Boasting" or "glorying" occupies a major section of chapters 10—11. In what will Paul boast, and in what does he refuse to boast? (10:15–18)

What is the folly Paul reluctantly engages in? (11:1, 16–19)

What fear pushes Paul to do what he finds so distasteful? (11:2–3)

What unique role does Paul play in bringing the Corinthians to Christ? (11:2)

WORD WEALTH

Godly jealousy: In 2 Corinthians 11:2, we see Paul's heart revealed. Paul feels "godly jealousy" for the Corinthians. He uses the Old Testament metaphor of Israel as bride and God as Bridegroom (Is. 50:1; 54:1–6; Hos. 1—3). In the New Testament, Jesus Christ is the Bridegroom and the church is the bride of Christ (Eph. 5:22–23). Using imagery we find in both Testaments, Paul talks about himself as if he were the father of a bride. In this case, Paul is the spiritual father of the Corinthians, who are the bride he wants to present to Christ at His second coming. When Paul led the Corinthians to Christ, they became engaged or betrothed to Him.

In contrast to marital engagement in modern secular society, a betrothal in ancient times was an agreement as sacred and binding as marriage itself. Any unfaithfulness on the part of the bride-to-be during this engagement period was considered adultery. In this case Paul is concerned about spiritual adultery and the Corinthians being seduced by "another Jesus," "a different spirit," and "a different gospel" (11:4).

What role do his opponents play regarding the Corinthians' relationship to Christ? (11:3, 4)

Verses 4 and 5 make clear that this conflict is not about whether or not some Corinthians and Paul's opponents think Paul has an unpleasant personality or is an uninteresting preacher. Instead, from the apostle's perspective, the conflict centers on the true gospel, the real Jesus, the genuine Holy Spirit.

 PROBING THE DEPTHS

What were the errors of the Corinthians who opposed Paul?

Second Corinthians shows how certain mindsets, certain ways of looking at things, directly oppose the gospel (2 Cor. 10:3–5). Have you ever known people who were ready to fight for pure doctrine, but whose spirit was critical toward others, self-centered, and ungracious? (See James 3—4 for an extended description of just such people—doctrinally straight, yet spiritually crooked because of proud self-will not submitted to Christ.) These practice serious error—errors of spirit more than of formal doctrine. This kind of error is quite different from the clear-cut doctrinal error that Paul opposed in his letter to the Galatians, yet it may be more dangerous because we easily overlook it while flourishing our doctrinal swords when "defending the faith."

What harmful mindset ("strongholds," "arguments," "thoughts" disobedient to Christ, 10:4, 5) prompted Paul to charge the erring Corinthians with promoting a different Jesus, spirit, and gospel? From careful study of both 1 and 2 Corinthians, we find that their error included wrong requirements for an apostle. More generally, they held to a view of spiritual leadership that Jesus rejected in His own ministry. This wrong view of leadership becomes more sharply focused for us as we summarize the reasons why some Corinthians and latecomer "apostles" judged Paul to be incompetent as an apostle. These claimed that Paul . . .

- *had questionable character,* evidenced by his vacillation in his travel plans ("We can't trust what he says he will do"; see lesson 1), by his weak personal presence contrasted with his strong letters ("He's either a flatterer or a wimp who won't talk straight to you in person."), and by his suspicious handling of the collection intended for the Judean saints ("He's dishonest.");

- *lacked the good references, strong personal presence, and eloquence in preaching* that were defining elements of a good leader ("Leaders should have sterling recommendations from other well-known leaders and must be commanding in their personal presence and entertaining in their speaking.");

- *lacked social standing and showed little promise for fitting in the local social scene* ("We want a leader who comes off well with the movers and shakers of our city. Paul is just a blue-collar tentmaker, and he has insulted some wealthy members in the church by refusing their offer of a financial gift. He's not very careful about his relationships with important people.");

- *lacked manifestations of the Spirit* ("Is Paul still Spirit-filled? We wonder. When he started the church, there were signs and wonders. But lately he's been pretty weak in this area, especially since he put tight controls on speaking in tongues in worship. [1 Cor. 12—14] Really, the apostles who've come to us recently seem so much more anointed. Maybe all these other problems are signs that he's lost the anointing. Our leader simply must have a strong anointing.").

How was this evaluation of Paul wrong? First were errors of fact: Paul's word was good, although he would change his plans when the situation justified it. He was not a flatterer or wimp. He had felt intimidated by the cultural elitism of Greco-Roman Corinth when he established the church (1 Cor. 2:1–3), and he preferred to resolve conflicts at the lowest level possible. But he would be as tough as the ministry mission required. The extent to which he endangered himself in his missionary journeys proved that. He did not mishandle the collection, and such accusations were baseless. On the contrary, the collection was being handled by representatives from each contributing church so there would be no question of impropriety.

The critics appear to be right on one point: Paul was not a trained orator, he lacked the dramatic presentation that training produced, and he admitted it. But substance was more important than style, and the Corinthians' own changed lives were all the "expert recommendation" he needed and proof enough that Paul had spiritual substance.

The critics were most wrong in what they assumed about Spirit-filled leadership. With their job description Paul came out a loser, but then Jesus would have as well. Why? Because they minimized the difference between life and leadership in culturally sophisticated but fully pagan Corinth and life and leadership in the new community established by Jesus—where the greatest is the least, where the leaders wear the towel of a slave and wash their followers' feet. The greatest error of Paul's critics lay in their worldly views of power, which they wanted to bring directly into church life without first passing them through the purifying fire of the example of Jesus, and Him crucified.

The conflict Paul dealt with in 2 Corinthians grows from the mindset he challenged in 1 Corinthians. There he attempted to center his new converts on the power of the Cross. They preferred the power of the Resurrection only and wanted to know Jesus only as the risen, ascended, exalted one. They had no interest in knowing Jesus also as the crucified one. For them, the Cross was merely one moment in the life and ministry of Jesus. They agreed that He died "for our sins" (1 Cor. 15:3), but the Cross had no other meaning for Christian life. What mattered were experiences of Resurrection power—signs and wonders, miracles, tongues, visions, and all kinds of exciting spiritual experiences.

The problem was not the Corinthians' belief in or experience of these manifestations. Paul also believed in and experienced such things. The problem was how they distorted the meaning of these manifestations. They distorted them by giving them too much value, while at the same time giving no value to the manifestations of "Cross power"—sacrificial patience, humility, endurance, and costly love that "suffers long and is kind, . . . does not envy, does not parade itself, is not puffed up; does not behave rudely" (1 Cor. 13:4–6). These manifestations of God's power shine through the ministry of Jesus and most brightly in His voluntary submission to the Cross.

In 2 Corinthians, Paul attempts again and again to help the erring Corinthians see and value these dimensions of God's power as much as they do those dimensions they associate with the risen, exalted Lord who is powerful among them in signs and wonders. Signs-and-wonders power is visible even to carnal people, and it is tempting to desire such self-evident power simply for selfish purposes, as Simon the sorcerer did (Acts 8). One mark of carnal Christians is their self-will, their grasping for power that they may use for themselves. This self-centeredness is manifested in their judgmental, unloving spirits, their impatience with those who do not always agree with them, their arrogance and insensitivity toward others. Truly Spirit-filled, Spirit-directed believers live a life of both the Cross and the Resurrection: The Cross life is manifested in their being crucified to their flesh and to the world. This is the continuing role of Christ's Cross in the Spirit-filled life, the cross He calls us to take up as we follow Him. Resurrection life is manifested in the things we typically call supernatural—signs, wonders, miracles, and so forth.

Anyone who looks at such manifestations of Resurrection life will agree that they are works of power. But people who do not see reality as God does will look at manifestations of Cross life and see only despicable weakness—a naked Jesus executed with two thieves by Roman legions; an unimpressive Paul enduring the hardships of travel and tribulation, making ends meet by tentmaking, so that he can proclaim this crucified Jesus as Lord and Christ.

The Corinthians who opposed Paul sought and acknowledged only those dimensions of divine power that appealed to them. Because they were carnal, only certain Resurrection-like manifestations of God's power appealed to them, and they discounted and despised all others. Humility, gentleness, hardship, endurance, patience—these struck them as things either to be avoided or of no merit, certainly not as manifestations of God's power.

Fixed as they were on only one kind of divine power, they judged leaders only on the single criterion of how well they manifested that kind of power in their ministries. Paul manifested that kind of power, to be sure, but not enough for the tastes of the Corinthians and less than the leaders who came to Corinth after him and sought acceptance by the Corinthians.

The harm with such a view? First, it distorted the gospel because it diminished the importance of the Cross. Second, it limited the ongoing experience of the gospel to only sensational experiences, thereby diluting the gospel so that it, in fact, lost much of its power. This diluted gospel would never bear the fruit of the Spirit (Gal. 5:22–26; it is no coincidence that the church at Corinth was rife with internal dissension; 1 Cor. 3—4). It could not create a community of loving, sacrificial believers. Third, this view would reject genuine gospel leaders and would choose flesh-pleasing performers instead. Finally, because it rejects Jesus crucified in favor of only Jesus glorified, it flirts with idolatry—remaking God in our image, an image that appeals to our preferences and contains nothing to challenge our sinfulness.

Because this Corinthian view was wrong and harmful, Paul minced no words in describing what these erring believers had done in accepting it (2 Cor. 11:4).

What skill does Paul admit he lacks? (11:5–6)

What in Paul's view more than makes up for any lack of rhetorical training? (11:5–6)

What behavior of Paul, comparable to that of Jesus, was held against him, according to 11:7?

BEHIND THE SCENES

Paul's craft of tentmaking (Acts 18:3) was held in low social esteem by Greeks. His financial independence was not intended to embarrass the Corinthians. Rather, he desired that they be "exalted" (lifted up) by his preaching the "gospel . . . free of charge."[1]

What do we know about the churches who helped support Paul when he was establishing the church at Corinth? (11:8, 9; 8:2)

Paul worked to support himself and received support from other churches. From whom did he not receive financial support while ministering in Corinth? (11:7–10)

How have some Corinthians interpreted and responded to Paul's refusal to accept local support? (11:11)

What reason does Paul give for not accepting local support while at Corinth? (11:12–13)

BEHIND THE SCENES

Patronage at Corinth

In order to understand 2 Corinthians 11:5–13, it is necessary to understand the ancient Greco-Roman practice of patronage relationships. As strange as it may seem to us, some at Corinth (probably opponents and the Corinthians sympathetic to them) accused Paul of not being a true apostle of God because he did not accept contributions from Corinth. Earlier, when he wrote 1 Corinthians, Paul acknowledged that the Lord "commanded that those who preach the gospel should live from the gospel" (1 Cor. 9:14). Yet he exempted himself from this command so that he could "present the gospel of Christ without charge" (1 Cor. 9:18). Rather than see Paul's self-support while their apostle as desirable, some Corinthians were insulted by Paul's refusal to accept their gift. The reason? To Paul, preaching the gospel free of charge kept him free of any obligations to "special interests" within the local congregation. He wanted to be the benefactor of the church, to be the father who willingly gave of himself to his spiritual children, not expecting to be repaid. But some of the Corinthians wanted to match Paul's gift of the gospel at no charge with their own gift. Apparently, they felt that not matching his gift by their own gift would leave them in a position of being Paul's social inferiors. This feeling makes sense when we understand the social context of friendship and gift-giving and -receiving.

In ancient Corinth, there were a variety of social relationships or "friendships" between people of different social status. A benefactor or patron would give money and other material benefits and expect to receive honor, praise, and other things in return. The recipients of these gifts would automatically be put in the socially inferior role—obliged either to assert their equality by a corresponding gift of the same or greater value or to accept their role as one who owed expressions of honor to their patron.

Did Paul simply resist the social role of a client because he was too proud? Or did his refusal come from his conviction about how the gospel should be provided free of charge? And did he also discern that the common Greco-Roman system of friendship, with its patrons and clients, fed arrogance and social divisions between the wealthier and the poorer, a system the gospel came to dismantle and divisions the gospel came to heal?

In any event, Paul's opponents used his refusal to accept support as proof that he was not a legitimate apostle. They argued that if he were a true apostle, he would have been worthy of such support and would have taken it, as any respectable teacher of the day would accept tuition from students.

What did Paul say that may explain why he refused support at Corinth? (1 Cor. 9:18, 19; 2 Cor. 11:10–12)

Review 2 Corinthians 11:1–13. Why does Paul call his opponents "false apostles, deceitful workers"?

For whom do such persons work, and what will be their end? (11:13–15)

FAITH ALIVE

This lesson includes one of the most important references to spiritual warfare in the New Testament, 10:3–5. How does what you have learned in this lesson shed any new light on your understanding of "strongholds," "arguments" that exalt themselves against God, and "thoughts" disobedient to Christ?

How has this lesson affected your understanding of the worldliness the church must combat?

What impresses you the most about Paul's situation with the Corinthians?

In what ways have you perhaps been applying worldly views to your life in Christ and within His church?

In what way does the Cross correct those worldly views?

How does God want you to tear down such strongholds and make such thoughts obedient to Christ?

---

1. *Spirit-Filled Life® Bible* (Nashville: Thomas Nelson, 1991), note on 2 Cor. 11:7.

Lesson 7/Wise Foolishness and Powerful Weakness
(2 Corinthians 11:16—12:9)

The job hunt is an American ritual. You prepare the best-looking resume you can with the most impressive wording to make your training and experience elevate you head and shoulders above the rest. Resume preparation guides tell you to

- Emphasize achievements, not just activities

- Maximize your strengths, minimize your weaknesses

- Avoid an arrogant tone, but list all pertinent honors, awards, and experiences in community service.

You know that on first reading, your resume may get thirty seconds, so you want to distinguish yourself from among all the possibly hundreds of other applicants for the position. You are competing with others for the position, perhaps only one will be hired, and you feel the need to make yourself look as good as you can without lying. A good resume is a socially approved form of boasting.

Paul found himself in an unwanted competition that required him to boast. He had been compared unfavorably against late-coming "apostles" who wanted the Corinthians to embrace them as their spiritual leaders. They had presented impressive resumes, complete with sterling recommendations from other leaders, and their in-person performances (they called it "ministry") pleased influential members of this congregation in Greece's entertainment capital. If a vote were taken, it looked sure that Paul would be defeated and turned out of office as the official apostle of Christ to Corinth.

Paul has another problem: he finds boasting not only distasteful but insulting to God. As he said in 2 Corinthians 10:17, all glorying (or boasting) is to be done only "in the Lord." That is, the only boasting any of us should do is boasting of our Lord and His achievements. If only the Corinthians and the false apostles saw the power of God in the Cross and boasted in it, then they would see the fullness of God's power at work in Paul and be reconciled to him. But because they are not reconciled, Paul is compelled to respond to the boasting competition. Does he then descend to the level of His opponents, even as he has claimed that he would not dare compare himself with them (10:12)? Or is he able to boast in such a way that all his boasting remains boasting in the Lord?

A Fool for You (2 Cor. 11:16–21)

Who wants to play the part of a fool? Some of the Corinthians look down on Paul and find him weak and foolish. Paul finds the boasting "according to the flesh" of their false apostles foolish. Yet, for the sake of the Corinthians, Paul is willing to be thought foolish and to do things he himself thinks foolish.

What is Paul doing that makes him fear others will think him a fool? (11:16)

Why is he boasting (11:1, 16), especially if he is not doing it "according to the Lord"? (11:1–2, 11, 12)

What is the tone of 11:19–21?

What kind of weakness does Paul admit to in 11:21?

BEHIND THE SCENES

Paul's reluctant boasting

It is difficult for contemporary Christians to understand Paul's references to "boasting" in light of the Bible's emphasis on such things as humility and the need not to be prideful. However, self-admiration and self-praise were the custom in Greco-Roman society as a means of building status. As the entertainment capital of Greece, Corinth hosted numerous games and oratory contests. Orators and debaters, who held the place that actors and rock groups do in our society today, came from around the ancient world to perform in Corinth's 14,000-seat theater. These masters of debate and rhetoric would often wear impressive clothing and jewelry and have elaborate hair styles.

The popular teachers and philosophers of the day used self-praise to develop a following and gain social power. Ancient authors Cicero and Plutarch wrote rules on the art of self-praise. In addition, the Sophists, orators who practiced an extremely showy form of oratory, developed a whole approach to self-praise and boasting in their rhetoric. In 2 Corinthians 10—13, Paul is specifically attacking those who were using the sophistic method of evaluating people and their public speaking skills. The criticism that Paul was not an effective speaker probably means that he did not use the techniques of the Sophists in his preaching and teaching. Judged by their oratorical theatrics, he came off as untrained. But apart from training in their methods, Paul also resisted the content of their speeches too, especially the speech of self-recommendation. Yet at this point in 2 Corinthians, he is so concerned about the inroads these false apostles have made, that he feels he must take them on directly and show their emptiness.

THE FOOL'S SPEECH (2 COR. 11:22—12:10)

Students of 2 Corinthians have labeled this section "The Fool's Speech," because it seems to be Paul's carefully crafted response to speeches of self-recommendation given by the false apostles at Corinth. In the Greco-Roman world, the speech to praise a person was called an encomium. It followed a traditional pattern. See that structure below, and then look up the portions of 2 Corinthians cited to discover how Paul's response relates to the original speech pattern we believe his opponents followed. Next to the verse listing, (1) summarize what the verses say, and (2) write how they follow or depart from the encomium pattern given in the left column.

Traditional Encomium	Paul's "Fool's Speech"
Narration of person's origin, family history, and birth *(They claimed to be Hebrews, Israelites, of the seed of Abraham, v. 22)*	v. 22
Achievements: *(From these topics, they would have listed items showing them to be outstanding servants of Christ, apostles)*	11:23–27
	vv. 28–31
a. Education/Pursuits	vv. 32, 33
b. Virtues	
c. Deeds	12:1–6
d. Blessings/Endowments	
	vv. 7–9a
Conclusion: Honor/Memorial	12:9b–10

Verses 9 and 10 provide the main point of Paul's speech. Look back over these verses, and for each unit, write how the experience(s) recounted in those verses shows Paul's infirmity or weakness:

11:23–27

vv. 28–31

vv. 32, 33

12:1–6

vv. 7–9a

Like today's modern resume, the self-praise of Paul's opponents would have emphasized the accomplishments they believed would show their audience how competent and successful their ministries have been. Rather than highlighting such accomplishments, what do all the items in Paul's speech have in common? (11:23—12:9a)

How does Paul's enduring such hardships show that he is a legitimate minister of Christ? (11:23–27)

How might Paul have written this part of his speech differently if he wanted to show that he performed more miracles, signs, and wonders than his opponents? (11:23–27)

A spirit of boasting, even over spiritual accomplishments, will create separation between those who boast the accomplishments and those who do not. Those who boast in such things will not want to identify with those they think are less spiritual than they. In fact, as 11:19, 20 shows, rather than identify pastorally with those less spiritual or less mature than they, Paul's opponents acted out their prideful arrogance in abusing the Corinthians. What does 11:29 show about how Paul relates to weaker, less mature believers?

The Roman army honored with a crown, the *corona muralis,* the first soldier who climbed up the wall of a city being attacked. How does this background information help you see how Paul "boasts" of his weakness in 11:32, 33?

From all we know about the Corinthians, it is plausible that some of them valued "visions and revelations of the Lord" highly and that Paul's opponents made much about these supernatural communications as, again, evidence of their superior apostleship. Paul responds to their boasting with some of his own, although with significant differences.

How does Paul play down his experience in 12:2, 3?

How does 12:4 show that such an experience had no value for ministry to others?

Paul's boasting is confined to an unnamed man who went up to the third heaven without knowledge of his state (in or out of the body) and who saw and heard things he cannot tell! Based on this summary of 12:1–5, what does Paul appear to think about the importance of such "visions and revelations" as credentials of true apostles?

Why will Paul not boast of anything concerning himself except his infirmities? (12:5, 6; 10:17, 18; 11:30)

When opponents boasted of visions and revelations, they boasted about experiences others could not witness. To the extent that people decided that such visions and revelations made Paul's opponents more spiritual than he, those who trust them are trusting assertions that cannot be verified. In 12:6, Paul invites the Corinthians to evaluate him and his ministry based on different criteria. What are they?

What does Paul acknowledge that he has received in "abundance"? (12:7)

But rather than these gifts encouraging him to boast of his superior spirituality, they are instead accompanied by what, given for what purpose? (12:7)

Who gave Paul both the revelations and the thorn in the flesh? (12:7)

 PROBING THE DEPTHS

What was Paul's "thorn in the flesh," and what do his three unmet requests show about his faith and about how we should pray in similar, seemingly unchangeable situations? (2 Cor. 12:7–9)

Because of some ambiguities, it seems very unwise to form dogmatic conclusions about certain particulars of this section. What is clear, however, is a **thorn in the flesh** (an intense, wearying difficulty or affliction) had come by means of a **messenger of Satan** (probably a demonically instigated assault). God's providence clearly allowed this (grammatically, a "divine passive," indicating God as the unseen Agent overseeing the entire process) that Paul might avoid being **exalted above measure by the abundance of the revelations.**

Though it is futile to try to identify the "thorn," it caused Paul great consternation and ultimately served a good purpose, becoming the occasion for a revelation to him of the overcoming **grace** of God, which proved **sufficient** in the midst of Paul's **weakness** (v. 9).

We must also note that though God does not respond to Paul's repeated pleading **that it might depart from** him by removing it, there is no indication God is upset with Paul for so pleading. In fact, Jesus' answer (v. 9) indicates God's concern to respond, howbeit differently than Paul had prayed. [Nor does Paul's repeated praying without receiving the answer he wanted show that he lacked faith. This passage emphasizes God's sovereignty in answering the apostle whose faith we often think of as looming larger than life, especially in the descriptions of signs and wonders that accompanied his ministry, according to Acts.]

Finally, it is important to note that Jesus' answer was not seen by Paul as punitive; nor did it cause him to resign himself to buffeting with a defeatist attitude. Rather, it affirmed in Paul that whenever Satan buffets him (either directly as the destructive adversary or indirectly as God's controlled agent to bring about character development) he can **boast in** his **infirmities** because Jesus' **grace** and **strength** will be **sufficient** to enable him to continue in his apostolic ministry. Neither the thorn, any messenger of Satan, nor any character-refining test from God will cause him to cease serving God. He can therefore **take pleasure . . . for when** he is personally **weak, then** he can be **strong** in Jesus.

Instead of the answer Paul wanted, what was the Lord's reply? (12:9)

WORD WEALTH

The mystery of the gospel of Jesus Christ and the secret of all ministry is wrapped up in the word *grace*. Jesus Christ told Paul, "My **grace** is sufficient for you," (2 Cor. 12:9). *Charis,* the Greek word for **grace,** comes "from the same root as *chara,* 'joy,' and *chairo*, to 'rejoice.' *Charis* causes rejoicing. It is the word for God's grace extended to sinful man. It signifies unmerited favor, undeserved blessing, a free gift."[2] Additionally, grace refers to God's motivating believers to desire and do His will, enabling them to persevere in doing God's will, with both the power and the endurance needed. Paul elsewhere capsulizes these dimensions of God's grace when he tells the Philippian believers that "it is God who works in you both to will and to do for His good pleasure" (Phil. 2:13).

From the preceding note, what sense of "grace" fits the words of Jesus to Paul? (12:9)

Compare the words of Jesus to Paul in 12:9c with 1 Corinthians 1:21–31. In what way is God's strength made complete, or expressed most fully, through what looks like utter weakness to the world?

How was God's strength expressed through the hardships Paul experienced? (2 Cor. 11:23–33)

Based on the Fool's Speech (11:22—12:10), explain as simply and accurately as you can the sense in which Paul is "strong" when he is "weak."

Students of 2 Corinthians consider the Fool's Speech to be a satire or parody of Paul's opponents' speeches of self-praise. Agree or disagree with this opinion, and explain why you take the position you do.

 FAITH ALIVE

In what ways do you see God's power expressed in the Cross of Christ?

How in your life can you see God's power expressed through your weaknesses or "infirmities"?

If signs and wonders were not Paul's priorities in ministry among the Corinthians, what were his priorities?

How do these priorities compare with your own in ministry?

What do you feel the need to understand more fully from this portion of Scripture?

Based on what you do understand, what changes in your perspective on ministry or your actions in ministry does this portion of Scripture direct you to make?

1. *Spirit-Filled Life® Bible* (Nashville: Thomas Nelson, 1991), note on 2 Cor. 12:7.
2. Ibid., 1766, "Word Wealth: 2 Corinthians 12:9, grace."

Lesson 8/Spirit-Filled Leadership
(2 Corinthians 12:10—13:14)

In the Jesus Movement of the mid-sixties to late seventies, God miraculously poured out His Holy Spirit upon the young people of our nation. Many young people who were converted "hippies" were called into leadership by the Holy Spirit. With little or no formal theological training, many of these people became effective ministers, evangelists, and Bible teachers. When they spoke, revival often broke out. Young people would repent of their sins, and many would accept Jesus Christ as their Lord and Savior.

What was the secret of their spiritual power? First of all, each of them had a profound personal encounter with Jesus Christ. They were deeply grateful for being saved and rescued from a path of destruction. Secondly, they were completely in love with Jesus Christ and would delight in spending time with Him in prayer and personal communion. Thirdly, they had a passion for God's Word and would spend hours studying the Bible. Finally, God gave them a shepherd's heart for those they led to the Lord, and they loved these new believers genuinely.

The result was that revival, evangelism, and discipleship was a natural outgrowth of the spiritual vitality that existed in their lives. Many of these people went on to receive a more formal theological training and began to mature as spiritual leaders. But at the core of their ministries was a passion for Jesus Christ and for walking in the fullness of the Holy Spirit.

Similarly, what enabled the early disciples and followers of Jesus Christ to turn the world upside down was not their affluence, education, or exceptional human abilities. These were ordinary people whose lives were dramatically changed through a personal encounter with Jesus Christ. In the same way today, when our lives are dramatically changed by Jesus Christ by the power of the Holy Spirit, we are able to become instruments of power which can transform the lives of others.

THE SIGNS OF AN APOSTLE (2 COR. 12:10–13)

Although Paul did not like to boast about it or "strut his stuff," he moved boldly in the supernatural gifts of the Holy Spirit when God directed him to do so. Paul was not preaching a merely intellectual gospel. Paul's ministry included, "signs and wonders and mighty deeds" (2 Corinthians 12:12). Paul stated in 1 Corinthians 4:20, "For the kingdom of God is not in word, but in power." In the ministry of Jesus Christ, the apostles, and in the lives of believers today, there should be a supernatural element to the preaching of the gospel. Yet according to Paul, the signs of a true apostle go beyond miracles. The miracles that God worked through Paul were done in the context of suffering, endurance, faithfulness in doctrinal matters, moral purity, accountability, and integrity of heart.

Read 12:10. How does Paul's statement here relate to the "signs of an apostle" (12:12), that is, the criteria for evaluating someone's claim to be an apostle?

Why did Paul boast like a fool? (12:11)

How does Paul differ with his opponents in evaluating the significance of "signs and wonders and mighty deeds"? (12:12)

What does the phrase "with all perseverance" mean in connection with the "signs of an apostle"? (12:12)

PROBING THE DEPTHS

Why did Paul not emphasize "signs and wonders and mighty deeds" among the Corinthians, as his opponents apparently did? (2 Cor. 12:12)

What many would list first in an assertion of spiritual authority, Paul mentioned last and did not elaborate, since the Corinthians had witnessed them.[1] Paul's opponents would have made much more of such spiritual manifestations, although it is questionable whether or not the Corinthians had themselves witnessed such manifestations through the opponents. Because the opponents relied so much on the recommendation of others and on their own self-recommendation, it is likely that they reported more signs and wonders than the Corinthians actually witnessed firsthand (12:6). In addition, the unhealthy, imbalanced exaltation of signs and wonders by some Corinthians caused Paul to de-emphasize them in order to help this church find balance.

What is the only way in which Paul treated the Corinthian church differently, compared to others he founded? (12:13)

How did Paul justify this different treatment? (12:14–16)

A complaint against Paul expressed earlier in the letter reappears in 12:16–18. What is that complaint, and how did Paul answer it?

BEHIND THE SCENES

"I caught you" (2 Cor. 12:16).

Paul echoes an accusation that he had tricked the Corinthians by sending others (**Titus** and the unnamed **brother**) to get their money (supposedly for Jerusalem), which Paul was keeping for himself. He refutes the charge by citing the character of his envoys, whom the Corinthians know to be honest (see 2 Cor. 8:6, 16–24).[2]

BEHIND THE SCENES

The marks of genuine spiritual leadership.

The Corinthians had some pretty worldly ideas in assessing leadership. Their ideas about power and authority came from the surrounding pagan culture and were not truly biblical. One of the reasons the so-called "super apostles" and false teachers were able to get such a foothold in Corinth is because they fit the worldly image of what a strong leader was supposed to be. In short, they used false criteria in judging leadership. They were looking for leaders with natural charisma, charm, strong rhetorical skills, and engaging testimonies about their supernatural experiences. Paul spared no effort, including playing the part of a fool, in order to get them to see that genuine spiritual leadership followed the servant-model of Jesus Christ, which emphasized self-sacrifice, humility, and identification with the weak and needy as much as works of power. For Paul, as for Jesus, there was no either-or choice: either works of power or servant-leadership character. Instead, both, in the proper relationship, characterized authentic apostolic leadership.

A spiritual leader must have the right motives in leadership. The apostle Paul was never self-serving. His constant desire was to please God and serve His church. As such God could trust Him with a difficult and important ministry. What does Paul identify as his motive for ministry? (12:19)

 FAITH ALIVE

Our inner motives in ministry are extremely important to the Lord. How do you think the purity of our motives affects our spiritual authority?

What prayer request in Psalm 19:12 asks God to help us keep our motives pure?

When we humbly walk before the Lord, how does a Holy Spirit-inspired confidence regarding our motives in ministry give us inner strength in facing opposition?

Where in 2 Corinthians do you find Paul expressing or implying how his clear conscience regarding both his motives and his behavior in ministry help strengthen him in the face of adversity in everyday life, from people, and from Satan? List a reference from at least three different chapters, and summarize what each reference says.

What, if anything, do you need to do to cleanse your conscience and purify your motives for ministry so that you can serve more effectively and with greater strength in the face of all kinds of opposition?

Looking Forward to a Third Visit
(2 Cor. 12:20—13:14)

Like modern pastors and spiritual leaders, Paul had to deal with problems in the church. He couldn't ignore them or sweep them under the carpet. In order to be the spiritual leader God called him to be, Paul had to confront the sin in the Corinthian church, discipline them spiritually, and exhort them to live pure and holy lives. Like many of our churches today, the Corinthians had allowed the corrupt values and practices of the surrounding pagan culture to pollute their lives. Paul was zealous to see spiritual health restored to the church at Corinth and he knew this could only happen if the people repented of their sins and allowed the Holy Spirit to sanctify them.

What two main kinds of sin did Paul fear still awaited his correction on his third visit? (12:20, 21)

BIBLE EXTRA

Compare the list of sins in 12:20, 21 with the list of the "works of the flesh" in Galatians 5:19–21. How are the two lists similar, and how different?

Paul regards his third visit as meeting what requirement for meting out further discipline to the disobedient among the Corinthians? (13:1; see also Deut. 19:15)

BEHIND THE SCENES

Weak in Him, but strong with them (2 Cor. 13:3).
Those who think Paul is **weak** (see 10:10) will find that he really does speak with the authority of Christ, who was able to be weak enough to be **crucified** and yet be the ultimate example of **the power of God.** Likewise, Paul can be **weak in Him** and at the same time powerful in acting and speaking as Christ's apostle in dealing with the Corinthians.[3]

Paraphrase 13:4 so that it speaks directly to what Paul will do when he visits a third time, if he finds as many disobedient as he fears.

In examining themselves, what from chapters 10 through 13 would Paul say was most important in showing whether or not the Corinthians are "in the faith"?

Even if to some Corinthians Paul still did not measure up as an apostle, what did he urge them to do nevertheless? (13:7)

What constraint on spiritual authority—and also a sign that such authority is genuine—is expressed in 13:10?

In what sense were the Corinthians not yet complete? (13:9, 11)

WORD WEALTH

Complete (2 Cor. 13:9), *katartisis* (kat-*ar*-tis-is; Strong's #2676), is related to the verb *katartizo,* which is used in Matthew 4:21 for the mending of the disciples' fishing nets. When used of humans, it includes the idea of making repairs or the necessary adjustments to bring one to full health, usefulness, or integrity. Helping one become complete involves the actions of equipping, disciplining, training, and improving.[4]

FAITH ALIVE

Read 2 Corinthians 13:3–9, in which Paul sums up the essence of "ministering in the Spirit and strength of Jesus." After reading these verses, spend some time in prayer before the Lord, and allow the Holy Spirit to search your heart. Then respond to the following items.

Consider each of the following areas, and write down any ways in which the Holy Spirit is leading you to crucify your flesh:

Your desires—

Your goals—

Your dreams—

Your plans—

Then allow the Lord to speak to you about what He may want to change or resurrect in your life. Allow yourself to experience a freeing transformation. Surrender your life with its plans, purposes, and pursuits into His hands, not out of fear or some sense of morbidity, but with the trusting confidence a young child has toward his loving father. Expect that when you release your life to Him that He will bless you and purify your desires. Expect that God will reveal to you His blessing and goodness, even though He may require some changes. Then write down what you feel the Lord has said to you about your life and ministry. His desires for you may be exactly what you have already written down above or He may be speaking to you about a new direction.

What do you feel are God's desires for you?

What do you believe are God's goals for you?

What do you believe are God's dreams for you?

What do you believe are God's plans for your life and ministry?

Finally, spend some time rejoicing in what God has revealed to you.

Then act upon what God has said to you in faith, fully expecting His miracle provision, guidance, and blessing.

Whether you are a layperson or a vocational minister, remember the words of Paul when he said, "Fulfill your ministry." (2 Tim. 4:5)

Do not allow what the Lord has told you to dissipate. Write down specific things the Lord has told you to do. Let these things be an action plan from God to you. Write them down in a place where you can review them regularly, and act on each one of them.

Compare 13:11–14 with 1:1–11 and its coverage in lesson 1. Identify terms and emphases common to both, and describe how the last few verses relate to the first eleven in the book.

You have now reached the end of the study of this important letter that is studied far less often than its companion, 1 Corinthians. Second Corinthians shows us genuine apostolic leadership under fire, leadership that consciously seeks to pattern itself after Jesus Christ. It is helpful to pull together some main emphases from the letter.

What caused Paul to be unattractive in the eyes of those Corinthians who favored following Paul's opponents?

What was it these Corinthians liked about Paul's opponents?

How did Paul's ministry express the Spirit and strength of Jesus in ways his opponents did not?

FAITH ALIVE

How has your study of 2 Corinthians helped evaluate the extent to which your own ministry expresses the Spirit and strength of Jesus?

What most surprised you about Paul's ministry, his struggles with the Corinthians, or about his opponents' appeal to some Corinthians from this study?

How is that discovery pertinent to your service in ministry?

How is that discovery pertinent to your cooperation with those the Lord has placed in spiritual authority over you?

From what he said in 2 Corinthians, what advice do you think Paul would give to a local church that is becoming dissatisfied with the ministry style of their pastor and is looking for someone "a little more dynamic, a little more anointed"?

In your own words and after reviewing all of 2 Corinthians, put "in a nutshell" what Paul most wanted the Corinthians to understand were the most reliable indicators that one in fact ministered in the Spirit and strength of Jesus:

1. *Spirit-Filled Life® Bible* (Nashville: Thomas Nelson, 1991), note on 2 Cor. 12:12.
2. Ibid., note on 2 Cor. 12:16.
3. Ibid., note on 2 Cor. 13:3.
4. Ibid., adapted from 1767, "Word Wealth: 2 Cor. 13:9, complete."

Lesson 9/Qualifications for Leadership in Ministry
(1 Timothy 1—3)

Many of us have had the experience of sitting quietly in our homes when the doorbell rings. When we answer the door, we discover two strangers there supposedly to tell us about Jesus Christ. Yet after we listen for a few minutes, we get the distinct impression that the Jesus they are talking about is not the Jesus we know. The people at our door are talking about "another Jesus" and "another gospel," terms we met in 2 Corinthians 11.

Whether through cultists at our doorstep or by some Hollywood celebrity talking about their guru or some new religion they have discovered, our society is filled with people who are talking about "another gospel," and "another Jesus" than the one the Bible talks about. They may use the words "Jesus," "the Son of God," "miracles," and the like, but they are not talking about the God of the Bible. Some of these people claim to have had supernatural experiences in which they have supposedly died and gone to heaven and talked with God. Others have met with angels or aliens or have had out-of-body experiences in which they received spiritual revelation.

Unfortunately, spiritual deception exists not only in our secular culture, but also inside the church. The apostle Paul had to deal with false teachers who were preaching "another Jesus," "another gospel," and who were of "another Spirit" than the Holy Spirit. This is why in 2 Corinthians, 1 and 2 Timothy, and Titus, he stressed the need for sound doctrine. The teaching of solid biblical doctrine is one of the best ways we prevent spiritual deception from entering the church.

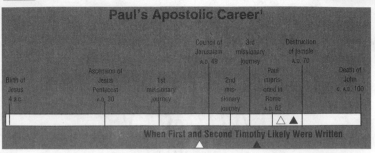

THE PASTORAL EPISTLES

Along with Titus, 1 and 2 Timothy belong to a group of Paul's writings which are called the Pastoral Epistles. The reason they are called the Pastoral Epistles is because they were written to two of Paul's spiritual sons, Timothy and Titus. Timothy was pastor of the church of Ephesus, and Titus was responsible for the church on the island of Crete. In Paul's letter to Timothy, which was written around A.D. 64, Paul instructs Timothy in matters such as the removal of false doctrine, public worship, and church leadership. In a very real sense, the epistle of Paul to Timothy is a practical "Handbook for Pastors."

BEHIND THE SCENES

The Pastoral Epistles
The Pastoral Epistles (1 and 2 Tim., Titus) were written by the apostle Paul. The primary purpose of 1 Timothy was to encourage Timothy in his difficult job of dealing with false doctrine as well as to give instruction concerning his role as a pastor and church leader. In addition, Paul outlined the responsibilities and duties of those in church leadership. Many Bible scholars believe that this epistle was written after Paul's first Roman imprisonment. After his release from prison, Paul ministered for a number of years and then was

arrested again when the emperor Nero began to launch persecution against the church. Finally, Paul was executed for his bold stand for Jesus Christ—possibly by being beheaded. The events in the Pastoral Epistles took place during this period of freedom between Paul's two imprisonments. The apostle Paul maintained a vibrant faith in the midst of severe trial, persecution, imprisonment, and eventually martyrdom.

 ## BEHIND THE SCENES

Error and Heresy in the Early Church

When we read the Pastoral Epistles, we see that spiritual error and heresy was a problem for the churches at Ephesus and Crete. When Paul talked about "fables and endless genealogies" (1:4), he was talking about the ancient practice of inventing romantic and fictitious tales tracing the historical background of cities and families back to the gods. The ancient world was fascinated with genealogies. Men like Alexander the Great paid to have a pedigree constructed tracing his forefathers back to mythological figures like Achilles and Hercules. The ideas that gave birth to full-blown Gnosticism in the second century were influential in Paul's time, including "fables" and "genealogies."

The danger of Gnostic ideas lay not in their fictitious accounts of man's origin, but in their promotion of two very dangerous false beliefs. Gnosticism taught that matter and the body are evil, and only non-material spirit is good. Ironically, this false teaching produced two opposite types of behavior: a libertinism ("all things are permissible") and a false asceticism ("touch not, handle not"). Some Gnostics forbade people to marry and advocated strict dietary laws. These taught that a person should completely deny his or her body through harsh and rigorous self-denial and discipline. Since the Gnostics taught that the body did not ultimately matter, others took this idea as a license to indulge in complete immorality.

Both of these ideas are unbiblical and can cause serious spiritual harm. Many of the Gnostic ideas are found in what is called the New Age movement, mysticism, and the cults. In addition, Gnostic, heretical ideas have been introduced into some areas of the church. Excessive legalism, with its long lists of "do's" and "don'ts" and an inordinate emphasis on fleshly means to place the body under subjection, can be Gnostic. Also Gnostic are forms of "super spirituality" in which visions, dreams, ecstatic, and supernatural experiences are prized, while the ordinary responsibilities of life are despised. Such false spirituality pits the supernatural against the natural, God's good creation against God's redemption, and being spiritual against being human. It undercuts itself, devalues creation, and leaves little to be redeemed.

After considering this description of Gnostic belief and its relationship to false doctrine, write down some examples of modern spiritual error or current unbalanced teaching that may be Gnostic in its influence.

FALSE PROPHETS AND FALSE TEACHING (1 TIM. 1:3–20)

Read Paul's discussion of false prophets and false teaching in 1 Timothy 1:3–29, and answer the following questions.

Why did Paul exhort Timothy to remain in Ephesus? (1:3)

How does false doctrine produce disputes? (1:4)

What is the purpose of God's commandment? How do false teachings betray their origin? (1:5, 6)

What is one of the motivations of false teachers? (1:7)

What kinds of sin and immorality are contrary to sound doctrine? (1:10)

In response to the spread of false doctrine, what did Paul exhort Timothy to do? (1:18)

THE MINISTRY OF INTERCESSION (1 TIM. 2:1–8)

One of the most important ministries of the local church and of individual Christians is the ministry of intercessory prayer. So important is this ministry that Paul starts off his discussion on intercessory prayer with, "I exhort first of all that supplications, prayers, intercessions, and giving of thanks be made for all men" (2:1). In this passage of Scripture, the church is given the responsibility to intercede and pray for local, state, and federal governmental leaders, the heads of industry, the media, the school systems, the courts, and "all who are in authority" (2:1). Paul is saying that there is a direct relationship between the quality of life in our communities, cities, and nation and the quality of our intercessory prayer life.

Distinguish the following terms from each other:

Supplications (2:1; see also Phil. 4:6)

Prayers (2:1)

Intercessions (2:1)

Giving of thanks (2:1)

WORD WEALTH

Supplication is more than petitioning, but suggests an intensity of earnestness in extended prayer—not to gain merit by many words, but to fully transfer the burden of one's soul into God's hands. Prayer and peace are closely connected. One who entrusts cares to Christ instead of fretting over them will experience the peace of God to guard him from nagging anxiety.[2]

Why does Paul tell us to pray for "all who are in authority"? (2:2)

What does God want from this type of prayer? (2:4)

 PROBING THE DEPTHS

In addition to worship, making disciples, teaching the Word, evangelism, and fellowship, one of the key ministries of the local church should be intercessory prayer. In recent times, we have seen the Holy Spirit revive this much-needed focus on intercessory prayer. If Christians wish to see good government, the healing of our homes, communities, cities, and nations, prayer, fasting, and intercessory prayer is the biblical key. The power of intercessory prayer is that it recognizes that the primary warfare is spiritual and takes place in the invisible realm. Prayer, fasting, and intercessory prayer allow the church to unleash powerful spiritual weapons that have the capacity to effect real change in our world.

Why did Paul make the statement "first of all that supplications, prayers, intercessions, and giving of thanks be made"? (2:1)

Using contemporary terms, who are the people we should be praying for? (2:2)

What are we to expect when we pray and intercede? (2:2)

Explain what the term "without wrath and doubting" means in relationship to intercessory prayer? (2:8)

What does the term "without wrath and doubting" say about the relationship between unity and the release of spiritual power? (2:8)

WOMEN AND MINISTRY IN THE CHURCH (1 TIM. 2:9–15)

Read Paul's instruction in 2:9–15 concerning what seems to have been a local church problem in ancient Ephesus.

 PROBING THE DEPTHS

Can a Woman Serve in Ministry? (1 Tim. 2:9–15)

Women in the ministry is a hotly debated issue in some quarters of the Christian community. There are some who see Paul's statement, "And I do not permit a woman to teach or to have authority over a man, but to be in silence" (2:12), as a clear prohibition against women in the ministry. But this Scripture must be taken in the greater context of the entire Old and New Testaments. In the Old Testament, some of Israel's finest leaders were women, such as Deborah the judge. Second, in the New Testament, women like Phoebe (Rom. 16:1) and Philip's daughters (Acts 21:9) were involved in ministry. In addition, in Philippians 4:2, Chloe and Euodia appeared to have leadership roles in their fellowships.

Hayford's Bible Handbook says, "It is puzzling why the place of women in ministry is contested by some in the church. Women had an equal place in the Upper Room awaiting the Holy Spirit's coming and the birth of the church (Acts 1:14). Then Peter's prophetic sermon at Pentecost affirmed the Old Testament promise was now realized: 'your daughters' and 'maidservants' would now share fully and equally

with men in realizing the anointing, fullness, and ministry of
the Holy Spirit, making them effective in witness and service
for the spread of the gospel."[3]

For those who might think that this viewpoint is merely an
accommodation to the thinking of our contemporary culture,
Hayford's Bible Handbook adds, "The acceptance of women in
a public place of ministry in the church is not a concession to
the spirit of the feminist movement. But the refusal of such a
place might be a concession to an order of male chauvinism
unwarranted by and unsupported in the Scriptures. Clearly,
women did speak—preach and prophesy—in the early church."[4]

The Spirit-Filled Life® Bible notes that "the prohibition of
v. 12 refers to the authoritative office of apostolic teacher in
the church. It does not forbid women to educate, proclaim
truth, or exhort [prophesy]."[5]

If a woman is clearly gifted in ministry and has demonstrated the kind of character that the Bible requires for leadership, should she be allowed a place in public ministry? Why?

By not allowing women who are called by God to minister, what harm can be done to the body of Christ?

How can suppressing women from ministry hurt our witness before a watching world?

How can a wrong view of women in ministry actually prevent some people from accepting Christ as their Savior?

QUALIFICATIONS OF CHRISTIAN LEADERS (1 TIM. 3:1–13)

In 1 Timothy 3:1–13, Paul outlines the qualities that
should characterize any Christian leader. Unlike our secular
society, which in many cases is willing to overlook the moral
character of a man in a position of leadership, the Bible teaches
that there is an inseparable link between a man's moral character and the ability to lead effectively. In addition, the Bible
teaches that a Christian leader must be able to manage his own

home well (3:4–5, 11, 12). How a man treats his wife is a good indication of how he will treat the "bride of Christ" or the church. The quality of a man's marriage and family life will reflect his ability to lead the church. This does not mean that a Christian leader must have a perfect home life. But it does mean that he can "rule his own house well" (3:4).

Briefly define the fifteen qualities of a Christian leader outlined by Paul in 1 Timothy 3:1–5:

1. "blameless"

2. "the husband of one wife"

3. "temperate"

4. "sober-minded"

5. "of good behavior"

6. "hospitable"

7. "able to teach"

8. "not given to wine"

9. "not violent"

10. "not greedy for money"

11. "gentle"

12. "not quarrelsome"

13. "not covetous"

14. "one who rules his own house well"

15. "having his children in all submission with all reverence"

BEHIND THE SCENES

The Position of a Bishop

The Greek word for bishop, *episkopos,* refers to someone in local pastoral oversight. The term "bishop" is not the monarchical episcopate of ecclesiastical authority which came later in church history. The word "bishop" translated today would simply mean pastor or elder (Acts 20:28; Titus 1:5–9; 1 Peter 5:1–2). A better word for "bishop" would be "supervisor" or "overseer." *Episkopos* was a Greek term for men who were appointed to regulate the affairs of a city. Two things characterized *episkopos:* (1) oversight over a particular work; (2) accountability to a higher power or authority. This definition gives us insight into the spiritual authority God has given the local pastor. The local pastor has been given charge by God not only for his congregation, but also for the spiritual condition of the community or city in which he lives.

   PROBING THE DEPTHS

A "One-Woman Man" (1 Tim. 3:2)

The term "the husband of one wife" is not solely referring to polygamy. In Ephesus, polygamy was not a real problem and was uncommon in Roman culture. In Roman society, as in our modern-day culture, polygamy was really unnecessary because of easy divorce laws and widespread sexual permissiveness. The actual Greek translation of "the husband of one wife" literally means a "one-woman man." Thus, the Christian leader must be a man who is faithful to his one wife, both mentally and physically.

Look up the following Scriptures, and write what they mean to you in terms of Paul's admonition that ministers be a "one-woman man" (3:2).

Job 31:1

Matthew 5:27–28

Proverbs 5:1–23

FAITH ALIVE

Which of the qualifications for spiritual leadership do you already fulfill?

For which do you want to grow so that you may become better fit to serve as God has called and equipped you?

1. Jack W. Hayford, *Hayford's Bible Handbook* (Thomas Nelson Publishers, 1995), 409.
2. *Spirit-Filled Life® Bible* (Nashville: Thomas Nelson, 1991), note on Phil. 4:6, 7.
3. *Hayford's Bible Handbook*, 793.
4. Ibid.
5. *Spirit-Filled Life® Bible*, note on 1 Tim. 2:12.

Lesson 10/Fighting the Good Fight of Faith (1 Timothy 4—6)

The whole world was watching when Evander Holyfield and Mike Tyson entered the boxing ring. Through pay television and satellite hundreds of millions of people gathered in living rooms, theaters, and sports arenas to watch the fight for the "Heavyweight Championship of the World." The fight was fierce, but Evander Holyfield finally pulverized Tyson, the titleholder.

Holyfield, who testifies to being a committed Christian, used the global platform that he had been given as champion to share his testimony in Jesus Christ. Major newspapers, television networks, and national magazines reported Holyfield's commitment to Jesus Christ. Not only had Holyfield fought a good fight, but he had won! He had defeated the formidable Mike Tyson in the ring. If he had not fought and won, then the world would not have paid attention to Evander Holyfield's testimony about how Jesus Christ has changed his life.

The apostle Paul told believers in Jesus Christ to "fight the good fight of faith" (1 Tim. 6:12). Christianity was never meant to be a passive spectator sport. Every Christian must enter the ring of life and be prepared to fight spiritually. The wonderful thing about this spiritual battle is that in the end we cannot lose. We may suffer temporary defeats, setbacks, and even failure. But as Paul said in Romans 8:37, "Yet in all these things we are more than conquerors through Him who loved us."

Through the blood of Jesus Christ we can be completely cleansed of failure. We can stand up and fight spiritually even if we have been temporarily knocked out. Through relying on the power of the Holy Spirit, we can receive new strength to "fight the good fight of faith" (1 Tim. 6:12). The "greater One" lives inside us, and He will lead us to victory. In the Christian life and in ministry, we often face struggles where it all seems hopeless. But as we draw upon His strength, we will discover the power to become champions.

Death did not defeat Jesus Christ. Paul was not bound by jail. David was able to slay a giant. Moses parted the Red Sea. Three Hebrew lads overcame a fiery furnace, Daniel lived through a den of lions, and Joseph did not yield to temptation. All of these accounts were written in the Bible so that we might learn that we can triumph and be victorious in Jesus Christ.

A Warning Against Apostasy (1 Tim. 4:1–7)

The apostle Paul very clearly warned that in the latter times, or last days, "some will depart from the faith, giving heed to deceiving spirits and doctrines of demons" (4:1). In a very real sense, we have seen spiritual deception increase in our time with things like the New Age movement, mysticism, cults, and other spiritual counterfeits running rampant in our society. Furthermore, we have seen an undermining of the historic Christian faith by liberal schools of theology, which have attempted to discredit the authority of the Bible and such things as the bodily resurrection of Jesus Christ. In an effort to "defend the faith," many have confronted spiritual error and championed biblical truth. However, two equally important dangers exist in this battle. The first danger is not confronting spiritual error and deception being spread by false teachers. The second danger is incorrectly labeling a minister or a teacher as a "false teacher."

How can we properly discern if someone is "giving heed to deceiving spirits and doctrines of demons"? (4:1)

How can we avoid the danger of falsely labeling someone as a false teacher? (4:2)

How can we be sure that we have cultivated "good doctrine"? (4:6)

PROBING THE DEPTHS

The Supernatural Dimension of Ministry (1 Tim. 4:12–16)
As a spiritual leader, Timothy was to combat the false teaching at Ephesus by teaching sound doctrine and exemplary moral conduct. However, Paul also calls attention to the supernatural aspect of Timothy's ministry in verse 14, which refers to the time when the elders of Iconium and Lystra laid hands on Timothy and prophesied over him concerning the gifts and callings that God had given him. The New Testament teaches us that there is the laying-on of hands with prophecy through which the Holy Spirit can direct and counsel a believer.

How can we properly exercise the laying-on of hands with prophecy today? (4:14)

In a church service, who should be allowed to do the laying-on of hands with prophecy? (4:14)

What are some of the guidelines that the Bible gives us regarding prophecy? (1 Cor. 14:29–32)

WORD WEALTH

Eldership (1 Tim. 4:14): The word eldership comes from *presbuterion,* which means "A body of elders (literally aged men) composed of men of dignity, wisdom, and maturity. The word is used both of the Sanhedrin (Luke 22:66; Acts 22:5) and of the Christian presbyters (1 Tim. 4:14).[1]

CARING FOR WIDOWS (1 TIM. 5:1–25)

True Christianity is not just about prayer, Bible study, worship, and evangelism. The early church was concerned about the practical needs of its people. Our society no longer looks to the church to take care of the poor and needy. We now have a massive state-controlled welfare system. In the early days of Christianity, the church looked after the spiritual and material needs of its people. The apostle Paul taught believers in Jesus Christ to be responsible and self-supporting as much as possible. In 1 Timothy 5:8 he says, "But if anyone does not provide for his own, and especially for those of his household, he has denied the faith and is worse than an unbeliever." Paul made a direct relationship between spirituality and the material concerns of life.

What did Paul say the church's responsibility to widows was? (5:3, 16)

When should the church not take care of widows? (5:4)

What did Paul say about young widows who were able to work? (5:11, 12)

How might this care relate to single parents today who work hard, yet live in poverty?

MINISTERS MUST BE ABLE TO EARN A LIVING (1 TIM. 5:17–20)

There is nothing more tragic than hearing stories about men and women who have served God as ministers of the gospel and who are forced to live in poverty when they retire. The apostle Paul makes it clear that the gospel of Jesus Christ is extremely practical. Those who serve as ministers, Bible teachers, and in other functions of the church should receive a suitable salary for their work. This means that ministers and their families should have such practical things as medical insurance, adequate housing, transportation, and even retirement plans.

Why do you think that Paul found it necessary to state "the laborer is worthy of his wages"? (5:18)

What did Paul mean when he said, "let the elders who rule well be counted worthy of double honor"? (5:17)

Why do you think that Paul included the words, "especially those who labor in the word and doctrine"? (5:18)

USE WISDOM IN ELECTING SPIRITUAL LEADERS (1 TIM. 5:1–22)

The truly New Testament style church promotes leaders wisely and uses appropriate discipline. In our culture today, the church often moves men into positions of leadership prematurely, especially if they have worldly success or fame. Such "celebrity" Christians often fall because they have been elevated into a position for which they are not spiritually ready. In our media-oriented society, this concept of leadership could be extended to any public platform such as singing ministries and television and radio ministries.

What is the danger in elevating someone to spiritual leadership too quickly? (5:22)

Tragically in our society, character is not as important an issue as it once was in political and business leadership. What does 1 Timothy 5:22 imply about the relationship between character and leadership?

THE IMPORTANCE OF ACCOUNTABILITY AND NEW TESTAMENT DISCIPLINE (1 TIM. 5:19–21)

In dealing with accusations against a Christian leader, Paul outlines a basic New Testament principle: "Do not receive an accusation against an elder except from two or three witnesses" (5:19). This provides a check and balance against false accusations and rumors which can arise against credible Christian leadership. When a Christian leader has sinned, public discipline is appropriate as a warning to others. The failure to exercise authentic New Testament discipline and to properly restore Christian leaders has often diluted the spiritual power and witness of the church. Before assuming any leadership position a candidate for spiritual leadership must be aware of the words of James: "My brethren, let not many of you become teachers, knowing that we shall receive a stricter judgment" (James 3:1).

If one person comes to us with a rumor or accusation about a spiritual leader, what should our response be? (5:19)

According to Paul, why is public New Testament discipline not simply optional? (5:20)

What problems might the failure to exercise New Testament discipline produce in the church?

What effect does this lack of discipline have on the witness for Jesus Christ in our society at large?

A WARNING AGAINST TEACHERS STIRRING UP STRIFE (1 TIM. 6:3–5)

Paul clearly taught that sound doctrine should be maintained and defended. He directly confronted the false teachers who were trying to undermine the gospel. However, Paul also warns that some leaders and teachers will fight over minor points of doctrine and simple differences of opinion. They will amplify and exaggerate theological disputes for the sake of furthering their careers, developing a following, and raising money. Paul is warning teachers to steer clear of "arguments over words," "strife," "envy," and "evil suspicions."

How can we discern the difference between someone who is defending sound doctrine and one who is trying to stir up controversy with impure motives?

How can we avoid entering into strife and dissension with our brothers in Christ when we simply have a difference of opinion?

What is the danger of crossing over the line from defending sound doctrine into simply stirring up strife?

SPIRITUAL LEADERS STAYING ON COURSE (1 TIM. 6:6–12)

The Christian leader is not supposed to be caught up in the world's value system of materialism and success. In reality, this important spiritual principle goes back to the Ten Commandments given to the children of Israel through Moses, "You shall not covet your neighbor's house; you shall not covet your neighbor's wife, nor his male servant, nor his female servant, nor his ox, nor his donkey, nor anything that is your neighbor's" (Ex. 20:17). The idea is that the Christian leader is not to seek after money, position, and power in his heart. Instead, he is to pursue "righteousness, godliness, faith, love, patience, gentleness." (6:11)

How does the "desire to be rich" create "many foolish and harmful lusts" which can produce personal destruction? (6:9; see James 5:1–6)

How does Paul define the "love of money"? (6:10)

PSYCHOLOGICAL REALITIES OF MINISTRY

Many people enter some facet of Christian ministry, either part- or full-time, with great enthusiasm and zeal. Then obstacles appear, stressful situations arise, people disappoint them, or rejection sets in, and the enthusiasm suddenly goes out the window. Depression, oppression, and discouragement replace joy. Things can get so bad that ministers feel like quitting their ministries. In addition, very real principalities and powers begin to take advantage of these genuine psychological forces, and all hell can break loose. This is why Paul told us to "fight the good fight of faith" (1 Tim. 6:12).

The apostle Paul specifically used the term "fight" (6:12). This term implies an often serious and violent conflict. How should the reality of this fight affect our personal preparation for ministry?

In what ways can we be prepared for obstacles and hindrances in ministry?

When discouragement, disappointment, rejection, and stress come against us, what should our response be?

Why should we not be surprised when adversity comes against us in ministry?

What is the source of our opposition? (Eph. 6:12)

 FAITH ALIVE

Spend a few minutes praying and seeking the Lord. Ask the Lord to shine His light into your heart and life. Ask Jesus Christ if there are any areas of covetousness in your life. Then ask the Lord to reveal to you any impure motives in your ministry. Are you in any way seeking money, position, or power, instead of His kingdom and His righteousness?

Is there anything in your heart which may be adversely affecting your ministry?

After you have spent a few moments in prayer, confess to the Lord any area in which you feel that your heart is not right or in which you have mixed motives. Ask Him to cleanse you of anything which displeases Him and to change your heart and purify your motives so that loving Him and loving others is top priority.

---

1. *Spirit-Filled Life® Bible* (Nashville: Thomas Nelson, 1991), 1845, "Word Wealth: 1 Timothy 4:14, eldership."

Lesson 11/Commitment to Ministry
(2 Timothy 1—4)

A leading national secular publication did an article on the rise of megachurches in America. The writer of the article talked about the fact that many of these new churches had done away with crosses, robes, spires, pipe organs, old hymns, hard pews, kneeling, and collection plates. Instead these super-churches of the future offer multimedia worship and view their congregation as customers. Many of the leaders of these new churches are attempting to reach a new generation, which they believe does not relate to the cultural settings of the past.

Whatever shape and form the church of the future takes, the key to its vitality and authenticity lies in how closely it adheres to the biblical model. Fortunately, God has given Christian leaders a handbook and blueprint for building the church—the Bible. In addition, the apostle Paul has timely instructions for those who lead God's people in today's society.

Customs and culture often change. There is nothing inherently spiritual about such things as pews, spires, and pipe organs. The first-century church simply met in people's houses. Although cultural aspects of the Christian faith can and do provide a rich source of inspiration to many people, some people can be reached only by different forms of religious style. In a culture which emphasizes the now and the immediate, we do not want to make the mistake of cutting ourselves off from our spiritual heritage and history. Many of the great hymns and traditional ways of doing things can provide for an abundance of powerful spiritual nourishment. At the same time we want to be open to new forms of worship the Holy Spirit inspires today.

The key to staying on course and building churches and ministries as God would have us build them is to be people who intimately know the Word of God and who pray and seek God's face with all our heart, soul, and mind. If we stay immersed in God's Word and follow hard after Jesus Christ, then whatever outward form the church takes will be guided by Him. After all, it is His church we are building.

2 TIMOTHY: A HANDBOOK FOR YOUNG MINISTERS OF THE GOSPEL

Second Timothy has been called a handbook for young ministers of the gospel. Paul wrote this letter to Timothy around A.D. 66 or 67 to give him instructions regarding the welfare of the church, its organization, and ways to safeguard the gospel. Second Timothy was not written from some theological ivory tower. Paul wrote this letter in chains (1:16) from the confines of a dungeon inside a Roman prison. With very little provision, Paul not only witnessed to his fellow inmates, but he also managed to write letters. At this time, Paul was passing on the mantle of his ministry to Timothy. In order to be the proper "spiritual father" to Timothy, he needed to confront something in Timothy's personality that could inhibit his full potential in ministry—Timothy's tendency to waver. This is why Paul exhorted Timothy with the words, "For God has not given us a spirit of fear, but of power and love and a sound mind" (1:7).

 WORD WEALTH

Sound mind (2 Tim. 1:7): One of the attributes that an effective Christian leader must have is ability to make the right decisions. A sound mind is essential in making this process work. The phrase comes from the word *sophronismos,* "which is a combination of *sos,* 'safe,' and *phren,* 'the mind'; hence, safe-thinking. The word denotes good judgment, disciplined thought patterns, and the ability to understand and make right decisions. It includes the qualities of self-control and self-discipline."[1]

Timothy, like many people in ministry today, was prone to fear and may have been reluctant to accept heavy responsibilities. As a true father in the faith, Paul dealt with these issues in Timothy's life and encouraged Timothy to exercise the principle of soundmindedness. After reviewing the definition of a sound mind, read 1:7 and answer the following questions:

How does fear inhibit our ability to make the right decisions?

How do the principles of power and love relate to our ability to lead others?

Why is having a sound mind essential to effective ministry?

Look up James 1:5–7 and Proverbs 3:1–26. Write how acting on the instructions of these Bible verses can help us develop a sound mind.

DO NOT BE ASHAMED OF THE GOSPEL (2 TIM. 1:8–12)

In our relativistic culture, there is constant pressure to dilute the power of the gospel. In addition, there is the ever present temptation to "dress up" the gospel or to wrap it in contemporary terms to make it more palatable to society around us. But the apostle Paul warns us against making such a mistake when he says that the "message of the cross" is "the power of God" (1 Cor. 1:18). In Romans 1:16 he writes, "For I am not ashamed of the gospel of Christ, for it is the power of God." In 2 Timothy 1:8–12, Paul repeats this message of not being shamed by the gospel. Although this message is foolishness to the world, it contains the power to save and transform peoples' lives.

As ministers of the gospel, what should our response be when people suggest that we tone down our message or make it more acceptable to a wider audience?

How can we avoid the temptation to be embarrassed by the message of the Cross and the power of God?

In a culture that often looks down upon preachers and evangelists, how can we maintain inner confidence and security about our call? (2 Tim. 1:11)

MODELS FOR STRONG MINISTRY (2 TIM. 2:1–6)

In writing about developing a strong ministry, Paul uses the metaphors of a soldier, an athlete, and a farmer. Read the following statements and explain in your own words how applying these principles can strengthen your ministry.

"Be strong in the grace that is in Christ Jesus" (2:1).

"Endure hardship as a good soldier of Jesus Christ" (2:3).

"No one engaged in warfare entangles himself with the affairs of this life" (2:4).

"If anyone competes in athletics, he is not crowned unless he competes according to the rules" (2:5).

"The hardworking farmer must be first to partake in the crops" (2:6).

RIGHTLY DIVIDING THE WORD OF TRUTH (2 TIM. 2:14–18)

Paul tells Christian leaders that they must "rightly divide" the Bible when they teach it. Paul compares the "word of truth" to a road being built which must be made straight. One of the responsibilities of ministers is to faithfully and responsibly present the truth of Scripture to the congregation. This means that we are not to bend what the Bible says, accommodate truth to whatever ideas are currently fashionable, or add to what the Bible says (Rev. 22:18).

Why does Paul tell Timothy to "be diligent to present yourself approved to God, a worker who does not need to be ashamed"? (2:15)

Why are we to "rightly divide the word of truth"? (2:15)

What might be some results if we are not faithful in communicating biblical truth?

How does unfaithfulness in teaching the Bible "increase to more ungodliness"? (2:16)

 PROBING THE DEPTHS

The Battle for the Bible

In the late nineteenth century, the acceptance of "higher critical" methods of studying Scripture developed first by a number of German theologians began to gain popularity among some Christian denominations here in the United States. "Criticism" of the Bible means analysis and interpretation. It is not, in itself, a negative term. Lower, or textual, criticism seeks to establish the most accurate Greek and Hebrew texts of the Bible from the thousands of partial copies of texts that have survived over the centuries. Higher criticism arises from lower criticism (actually, these terms are not used as widely now as they used to be), and it concerns itself with a number of questions, such as when did the events reported in this book occur, and when was the book written, by whom and why; what sources the writer used, how information was passed along from one generation to another before being set in Scripture; what written and oral forms Scripture comes to us in; and how the writer shaped the materials he worked with to create the biblical books as we have them.

Depending on the faith commitment of the Bible scholar, the various higher critical approaches can either root our faith more deeply in an historically accurate understanding of the world and words of the Bible, or they can be used to dismantle historic biblical faith. Faith is no friend of ignorance, and the proper use of many critical approaches has produced the study guides, Bible dictionaries, and commentaries that all Bible students rely on to help them "rightly divide the word of truth."

Unfortunately, however, much use of higher criticism has not so much enlightened as it has undercut the authority, divine inspiration, and inerrancy of the Scriptures. In the hands of scholars who do not submit their personal beliefs to the authority of God's written Word, these critical methods end up placing merely human opinions, ideas, and philosophies on par with or above biblical truth. When this happens, biblical truth is treated as only one classic opinion or tradition among many that educated moderns may consult in forming their personal truth. This approach to truth results, of course, in moral relativism and non-biblical ideas about God, man, sin, spirituality, and sexuality influencing the church. Consequently, certain quarters of the church have been robbed of their power to stand for holiness and biblical truth in the midst of a culture which is in a moral free fall. What we teach and believe matters in the real world because it has profound consequences in the lives of people. And wherever people resist God and His truth written in Scripture, they choose error for their guide.

How has moral relativism and accommodation within the Christian culture contributed to the moral and spiritual decline of our nation?

How does a strong view of biblical truth contribute to the strengthening of the family and the raising of godly children?

How can we communicate the absolute truth of the Bible without compromise, yet without succumbing to narrow sectarianism?

How can we hold up biblical truth and practice genuine Christian love simultaneously?

THE SANCTIFYING POWER OF THE SPIRIT (2 TIM. 2:19–22)

Paul states, "But in a great house there are not only vessels of gold and silver, but also of wood and clay, some for honor and dishonor" (2:20). The term "great house" refers to the church of God, the body of Christ. The idea is that believers and Christian leaders can determine if they will be honorable or dishonorable vessels in God's service. According to Paul, the key to being a "vessel for honor" (2:21) is to allow ourselves to be cleansed by the sanctifying power of the Holy Spirit.

The way we are to become sanctified is not through some program of trying to clean ourselves up or make ourselves pure. This can be a very subtle trap of the enemy, which leads only to inner frustration. Although Paul tells us to "flee also youthful lusts"—which involves more than sinful sexual desire—the emphasis is on pursuing "righteousness, faith, love, and peace" (2:22). We become sanctified by the power of the Spirit as we pursue and seek Jesus.

After reading 2 Timothy 2:19–22, write specific ways you can obey Paul's exhortation to pursue:

righteousness (2:22)

faith (2:22)

love (2:22)

peace (2:22)

Finally, how can we make sure that we "call on the Lord out of a pure heart"? (2:22)

WORD WEALTH

Sanctified: In 2 Timothy 2:21 the apostle Paul talks about being "a vessel for honor, sanctified and useful for the Master, prepared for every good work." The word *sanctified* comes from Greek *hagiadzo,* which means "to hallow, set apart, dedicate, consecrate, separate, sanctify, make holy. *Hagiadzo,* as a state of holiness, is opposite of *koinon,* common or unclean. In the Old Testament, things, places, and ceremonies were named *hagiadzo.* In the New Testament, the word describes a manifestation of life produced by the indwelling Holy Spirit. Because the Father set Him apart, Jesus is appropriately called the Holy One of God (John 6:69)."[2]

After studying the definition of sanctified, write a short description in your own words of how this work of the Holy Spirit can be produced in your own life:

MINISTERING IN THE LAST DAYS (2 TIM. 3:1–13)

When Paul uses the term last days (3:1), he is talking about the time from the first appearing of Jesus Christ until His second coming. The point Paul is making is that in the time period before the second coming of Christ, life is going to be increasingly difficult. In our day, we are seeing a significant rise in immorality, social chaos, economic upheaval, and the like. Yet it is precisely into that kind of world that God has both equipped and called us to minister the gospel of Jesus Christ. Through the power of the Holy Spirit, we have been strengthened to minister in "perilous times" (3:1). However, the last days are not only "perilous times" (3:1), but also the days in which God promises, "I will pour out My Spirit" (Acts 2:17).

In 2 Timothy 3:1–12, we are given a description of the kind of conditions that will exist in the last days. The following characteristics will characterize both men and women:

lovers of themselves	lovers of money	boasters
proud	blasphemers	disobedient to parents
unthankful	unholy	unloving
unforgiving	slanderers	without self-control
despisers of good	traitors	headstrong
haughty	lovers of pleasure	having a form of godliness
loaded with sins	led by lusts	denying the power of the gospel
cannot know truth	resist the truth	corrupt minds
evil men	impostors	deceivers

In a nutshell, these descriptions describe the kind of people who live in the dark world in which we have been called to minister. Briefly describe in your own words how the promise in Acts 2:17–21 makes it possible for us to minister in such a difficult and seemingly impossible situation.

FULFILL YOUR MINISTRY (2 TIM. 3:15–17; 4:1–5)

The foundation for successful ministry is a proper understanding of the divine inspiration of the Bible as our final authority in life. With that foundational truth in place, the man or woman of God must know the Holy Scriptures (3:13) so "that the man of God may be complete, thoroughly equipped for every good work" (3:17). It is from this foundation that we can "Preach the word!" (4:2), "endure afflictions, do the work of an evangelist, fulfill your ministry" (4:5). Indeed, the purpose for being established in the Word of God is to *completely fulfill your ministry.*

What difference does it make that "All Scripture is given by inspiration of God"? (3:16; see 2 Pet. 1:19–21)

What attitude and readiness might be required to "Preach the Word!" in good times and bad? (4:2)

In practical terms, what does "do the work of an evangelist" mean? (4:5)

Why is it important to God and to us that we fulfill our ministry? (4:5)

FINISHING THE RACE (2 TIM. 4:6–18)

About 30 years after his supernatural encounter with Jesus Christ on the Damascus Road, Paul was finishing the course that the Lord had set before him. Knowing full well that his life would be over soon, Paul gave some final instructions to Timothy and the church. Paul had offered up his life to God and was "being poured out as a drink offering" (4:6; see Num. 15:1–10). But Paul did not fear death. He said confidently, "there is laid up for me the crown of righteousness" (4:8). "Crown" translates the Greek word *stephanos*. A *stephanos* was the wreath given to winning athletes. Paul fully expected to be rewarded by God because He had been obedient to the call.

After reading 2 Timothy 4:6–8, briefly explain what you think Paul meant with the following phrases:

"I have fought the good fight" (4:7).

"I have kept the faith" (4:7).

"All who have loved His appearing" (4:8).

PROBING THE DEPTHS

The Abandoned Apostle (2 Tim. 4:9–16)

Not everyone had fought the "good fight of faith," "finished the race," and "kept the faith" (4:7) as Paul had. Some of those in ministry had dropped out or had become casualties along the way. One of Paul's closest associates, Demas, deserted Paul because he "loved this present world" (4:9). Perhaps Demas left Paul because the going got too tough. Maybe he had a shallow commitment to the Lord and was unable to make the sacrifice that ministry with Paul required. Mark had left Paul earlier (Acts 13:13; 15:36–41). However, Mark had changed and was restored to usefulness (4:11).

 ## FAITH ALIVE

From reading Paul's closing comments (4:9–21), we elicit a message about the need of all who are called into ministry and the Christian life itself. That message is "fight the good fight," "finish the race," and "keep the faith." Would you describe yourself today as a faithful soldier, a deserter, or a fearful or disheartened enlistee?

What personal lesson can you learn from Paul's discussion of Demas and his mention of Mark?

What do you need to do to become a more effective and faithful soldier?

What would you like God to do for you?

---

1. *Spirit-Filled Life® Bible* (Nashville: Thomas Nelson, 1991), 1853, "Word Wealth: 2 Tim. 1:7, sound mind."

2. Ibid., 1594–95, "Word Wealth: John 10:36, sanctified."

Lesson 12/Moral Character, Sound Doctrine, and Renewal
(Titus 1—3)

The fresh winds of Holy Spirit revival and renewal are blowing all over our nation and world. In his article "Seven Signs of Imminent Grace," Jack W. Hayford outlines seven "signals" seen in the church today that "indicate that our world is about to be flooded with the glory of God." These seven signs are "Miracles of Unity," "The Men's Movement," "Widening Worship Renewal," "Signs and Wonders," "Increased Prayer and Fasting," "Radical Reconciliation," and "Movement In Israel."[1]

Hayford and other church leaders such as Bill Bright, president and founder of Campus Crusade International, see evidence of both revival and evangelism all across our world. Such things as "Promise Keepers," the spirit of worship affecting all denominations and church traditions, the increase in signs and wonders, a renewed emphasis on prayer and fasting, racial healing in things like the 1994 "Memphis Miracle," and recent prophetic events in the nation of Israel all indicate that God is doing something unprecedented in our time.

The challenge for believers in such a time is to resist the pride that can come with being caught up with just what God is doing in our own small universe and to maintain a true interdenominational spirit. In addition, we are to be open to the "renewing of the Holy Spirit" (3:5), while at the same time teaching "sound doctrine" (1:9) and living "soberly" (2:11). If studying the revivals of the past teaches us anything, it is that the fires of revival can be extinguished and diminished through neglect and error. The key to extending revival is scriptural balance and openness to the fresh movement of the Holy Spirit.

BEHIND THE SCENES

Paul and Titus and the Work at Crete
Paul wrote his epistle to Titus around A.D. 64. Although there is no mention of Titus in the Acts of the Apostles, Titus was a close companion and valuable coworker of Paul. As a young preacher of the gospel, Titus traveled with Paul extensively and accompanied Paul and Barnabas to the Council of Jerusalem. Paul gave Titus the assignment of directing the young churches on the island of Crete. This letter to Titus gave him practical instructions concerning the performance of pastoral duties and the handling of difficulties and problems related to leadership.

The island of Crete was 160 miles long, situated strategically near Greece and Asia Minor. Titus had his work cut out for him. He had to deal with the "insubordinate, both idle talkers and deceivers" (1:10). In addition, the Cretans had a reputation for being "liars, evil beasts, and lazy gluttons" (1:12). The expression, "You Cretan" is still used today as a derogatory term.

LEARNING TO DELEGATE (TITUS 1:5–9)

One of the characteristics of a successful businessman, as well as spiritual leader, is the ability to delegate responsibilities to others. The downfall of many leaders has been their tendency to "micromanage" and their unwillingness to delegate. This principle of delegation is advocated by Paul when he says, "appoint elders in every city as I commanded you" (1:5).

Read Titus 1:6–9. Listed below are the qualifications described by Paul for elders or those in spiritual leadership. In your own words, briefly describe the meaning of each term:

QUALIFICATIONS OF SPIRITUAL LEADERS (Titus 1:6–9)	
blameless·	husband of one wife
having faithful children	not accused of dissipation
not accused of insubordination	blameless
a steward of God	not self-willed

not quick tempered	not given to wine
not violent	not greedy for money
hospitable	loves what is good
sober-minded	just
holy	self-controlled
faithful to the Word	teaches sound doctrine
able to exhort	able to convict those who contradict

DEALING WITH DISSENSION IN THE CHURCH (1:9–16; 2:15)

On Crete, certain Jewish legalists, "those of the circumcision" (1:10), were being insubordinate and teaching false doctrine. Every spiritual leader must be able to discern the people who will come into their church from time to time who are not in submission to any local church and who are insubordinate. These people love to hop from one church to another without calling any one church their home. Sometimes they justify their lack of submission to a local church and pastor by saying, "I am submitted to the whole body of Christ." Paul instructed Titus to deal with these disruptive people head on and to assert his pastoral authority.

Study the terms used by Paul below and briefly explain how this pastoral authority might be used today. Obviously, wisdom, diplomacy, and tact should be used in applying this authority. But these qualifications for how authority is exerted do not lessen Paul's exhortation not to simply "sweep these problems under the carpet," but rather to deal with them directly (Titus 2:15).

"By sound doctrine, both to exhort and convict those who contradict" (1:9)

"Mouths must be stopped" (1:11)

"Rebuke them sharply" (1:13)

"Exhort and rebuke with all authority" (2:15)

HOW TO LIVE IN THE LAST DAYS (TITUS 2:11–13)

Eschatology is the biblical doctrine dealing with "last things." Part of teaching sound doctrine is faithfulness in teaching about the return of Jesus Christ. Believers in Jesus Christ should never break fellowship about such things as the timing of the rapture of the church. Mature Christians can have different viewpoints as to the timing of such events as the rapture, the tribulation, and the Second Coming. Teaching sound doctrine requires that we teach such biblical themes as the Second Coming, the Millennium, the Great Tribulation, and other aspects of eschatology.

However, part of living "soberly" (Titus 2:11) in the time period the Bible calls the last days includes teaching responsibly on prophetic themes. Date-setting, conjecture, and excessive emotionalism surrounding the teaching of end time events can discredit the preaching of the gospel of Jesus Christ. There is nothing wrong with getting excited about the second coming of Jesus Christ, as long as this excitement does not become irresponsible or fanatical. The apostle Paul encouraged believers when he wrote that believers are to be "looking for the blessed hope and glorious appearing of our great God and Savior Jesus Christ" (Titus 2:13).

Of all people today, we should be most expectant and eager for Jesus' return as we note modern events and statistics. As I have written elsewhere,

> The greatest sign of all is that the gospel of the kingdom will be preached throughout all the earth, and this is precisely what is happening in our day in an

unprecedented manner. In fact, 70 percent of all world evangelism has taken place since the year 1900, and 70 percent of that progress has happened since World War II. It is interesting to note that the greatest explosion of world evangelism has happened since Israel became a nation again in 1948. All across the globe, millions are accepting Jesus Christ as their Lord and Savior as never before. Since the fall of communism in Russia, over thirty million people have come to Christ. In Communist China, over seventy-five million out of the one billion population have received Jesus into their lives.[2]

It is indeed spiritually sound to look for the "blessed hope and glorious appearing of our great God and Savior Jesus Christ" (2:13).

What sobriety and excitement should teaching on prophetic themes produce?

Why is it important to teach prophetic themes maturely, responsibly, and non-divisively?

What are the dangers of conjecture and date-setting regarding eschatology?

How is discipleship and godly living a vital part of teaching on the "blessed hope"? (2:12–13)

WORD WEALTH

Soberly comes from *sophronos,* which is from *sozo,* "to save," and *phren,* "the mind." This word is an adverb signifying acting in a responsible manner, sensibly, prudently, being in self-control and in full possession of intellectual and emotional faculties.[3]

The apostle Paul exhorts believers to live "soberly" (2:12). He is not talking about a dour-faced, legalistic, and joyless form of Christianity. He is telling us to live sensibly in an insensible age. This sobriety should be reflected in our teaching on such matters as eschatology and the Holy Spirit. Again, this does not mean that we cannot become excited or enthusiastic. Nor does it mean that we cannot be open to the Holy Spirit's moving in fullness and power. We can experience the fullness and renewing power of the Holy Spirit while at the same time being in "full possession of intellectual and emotional faculties."

The term "soberly" often conveys a negative message in today's culture. Briefly, write the attitude and action to which you are personally called by this term.

BUILDING A SOUND CHURCH (TITUS 2:1–10)

In this passage, Paul discusses a number of things which will contribute to building a strong church. Among these are exhortations that deal with the Christian family. "Sound doctrine" (2:1) will help to build strong families and a strong church.

Listed below are key characteristics of a sound church. Study the descriptions, and think of ways each would strengthen and build a sound church. Circle the four behaviors you would like your local church to cultivate. Present these to God in prayer, and ask Him how they might be accomplished. In cooperation with the leadership of your church, be ready to do what the Holy Spirit lays on your heart. Then put a check mark next to the behavior you most need to cultivate in your spiritual life. Submit yourself to the Word and to the opportunities God will bring for you to grow in this area.

CHARACTERISTICS OF A SOUND CHURCH
(Titus 2:1–10)

older men be sober	sound in faith	older women reverent
reverent	sound in love	not slanderers
temperate	sound in patience	not given to much wine
teachers of good things	wives be discreet	wives obey husbands
wives love husbands	wives be chaste	young men be sober-minded
mothers love children	wives be homemakers	ministers model good works, integrity, reverence
employees obey employers	employees don't steal	ministers model incorruptibility, sound speech

THE RENEWING POWER OF THE HOLY SPIRIT (TITUS 3:4–6)

Second Corinthians, 1 and 2 Timothy, and Titus all teach the importance of sound doctrine. But sound doctrine alone does not produce spiritual fruitfulness and revival, nor does just having the right doctrine build a church. There are many churches which seem to preach "sound doctrine" but have little life in them. This does not minimize the absolute importance of having sound doctrine. But a living church must also have the fresh move of the Holy Spirit in order to be all that Jesus intends it to be. In Titus 3:5 Paul used the phrase, "renewing of the Holy Spirit." He urged all believers to be constantly open to the fresh outpourings of the Holy Spirit "whom He poured out on us abundantly" (3:6). This involves a decision of our will. We must be truly willing to experience a fresh move of God's Spirit and revival.

How can we make sure that we are personally open to the "renewing of the Holy Spirit"? (3:5)

How can our own religious programs and routines actually block the fresh move of God's Spirit? (3:5)

What responsibility do we have as individual Christians and spiritual leaders to make sure that the Holy Spirit is continually being poured out abundantly in our midst? (3:6)

 WORD WEALTH

Renewing (Titus 3:5) gives us insight into ways we can participate in the Holy Spirit's renewal of our lives as individuals and churches. *Renewing* comes from the word *anakainosis,* which is a "combination of *ana,* 'again,' and *kainos,* 'new.' The word suggests a renovation, restoration, transformation, and a change of heart and life. In Romans 12:2, it indicates a complete change for the better, an adjustment of one's moral and spiritual vision. Here it stresses the work of the Holy Spirit in transforming the life."[4]

This definition is laden with concepts that can positively affect spiritual renewal. In your own words, briefly write what these defining terms can mean in your own life and ministry.

"new"

"renovation"

"restoration"

"transformation"

 FAITH ALIVE

God is sending His glory and revival all over our world today. How can we be sure that we are open to the revival He wants to do in our hearts without succumbing to pride or a loss of sound doctrine? How can we maintain openness for revival and renewal without surrendering to fanaticism or pure emotionalism?

As our world is being flooded with the glory of God, there seem to be many different streams of God's blessing and revival. How can we avoid the subtle pride that can occur by being preoccupied with what God is doing in our own church or movement to the exclusion of the body of Christ at large?

As revival comes, how can we protect a truly interdenominational spirit and avoid a "small-minded sectarianism"?

When we see an outbreak of unusual signs and manifestations, how can we avoid the trap of being excessively critical without losing our discernment?

1. Jack W. Hayford, *Signs of Imminent Grace* (Van Nuys, CA: Living Way Ministries, 1995).

2. Paul McGuire, *From Earthquakes To Global Unity* (Lafayette, LA: Vital Issues Press, 1996), 37.

3. *Spirit-Filled Life® Bible* (Nashville: Thomas Nelson, Inc., 1991), 1863, "Word Wealth: Titus 2:12, soberly."

4. Ibid., 1863, "Word Wealth: Titus 3:5, renewing."

SPIRIT-FILLED LIFE® BIBLE DISCOVERY GUIDE SERIES

*Coming Soon

SPIRIT-FILLED LIFE® KINGDOM DYNAMICS STUDY GUIDES

OTHER SPIRIT-FILLED LIFE® STUDY RESOURCES